MENTORS IN SCHOOLS

Developing the Profession of Teaching

edited by
Donald McIntyre
and Hazel Hagger

David Fulton Publishers
London

David Fulton Publishers Ltd
2 Barbon Close, London WC1N 3JX

First published in Great Britain by David Fulton Publishers 1996

Note: The right of Donald McIntyre and Hazel Hagger to be identified as
the editors of this work has been asserted by them in accordance with the
Copyright, Designs and Patents Act 1988.

Copyright © David Fulton Publishers

British Library Cataloguing in Publication Data

A catalogue record for this book is available from the British Library

ISBN 1–85346–411–2

Typeset by The Harrington Consultancy Ltd
Printed in Great Britain by the Cromwell Press Ltd., Melksham

Contents

The Report of a Programme of Research conducted by
Keele, Leicester, Manchester Metropolitan, Oxford, Sussex
and Swansea Universities and supported by the
Esmée Fairbairn Charitable Trust

Acknowledgements

The editors and authors wish to thank the Esmée Fairbairn Charitable
Trust for its generous and thoughtful support of the research work which
is reported in this book. We also wish to thank the many school-based
teacher educators who collaborated with us and upon whose thinking and
hard work this book is primarily based.

Contributors

Tony Bush is Professor of Educational Management and Director of the Educational Management Development Unit at the University of Leicester. His principal publications include *Theories of Educational Management* and *Managing Autonomous Schools: The Grant Maintained Experience* (with Marianne Coleman and Derek Glover). He is a member of the Continuing Professional Development Committee of the Teacher Training Agency.

Anne Campbell is Head of the Professional Development Programme at Didsbury School of Education, Manchester Metropolitan University. Her current research interests are mentoring, school-based teacher education and partnerships with primary schools.

Stephen Carney was Research Officer for the Oxford project reported in Chapter 6. His interest in school-based professional education comes from recent experience in the development of integrated work-place learning programmes for undergraduate students at the University of New South Wales. He is based in the Department of Educational Studies at the University of Oxford where he is continuing his research into the learning opportunities for mentors engaged in initial teacher education.

Marianne Coleman is a Lecturer in Educational Management and Director of the Distance Learning Unit in the Educational Management Development Unit of the University of Leicester. She is the co-author of *Managing Autonomous Schools: The Grant Maintained Experience.*

Lisa Dart is English Curriculum Tutor on the Secondary PGCE at the University of Sussex.

Pat Drake is the Secondary PGCE Course Director and Mathematics Curriculum Tutor at the University of Sussex.

Derek Glover, Research Fellow, Department of Education, University of Keele, was formerly head of Burford school, Oxfordshire but took early retirement in order to complete a PhD in school and community relationships. He has since become involved in teaching and research for Keele, Leicester and the Open University.

Hazel Hagger is Tutor for Professional Development in the Department of Educational Studies at the University of Oxford. For the past few years she has been engaged in research and development in mentoring, school-based teacher education and the induction of newly qualified teachers. Her recent publications include *Mentoring: Perspectives on School-based Teacher Education* (co-edited with Donald McIntyre and Margaret Wilkin), *The School Mentor Handbook* and *Managing Student Teachers' Learning* (both with Donald McIntyre and Katharine Burn), and *The First Year of Teaching* (with Andrew White).

Ian Kane is Head of the Didsbury School of Education, Manchester Metropolitan University. He is currently Chair of UCET (Universities Council for the Education of Teachers).

Donald McIntyre is Professor of Education at the University of Cambridge. As Reader in Educational Studies at the University of Oxford from 1986 to 1995, and previously at the University of Stirling, he was primarily concerned with research and development in teacher education and with research on classroom teaching. His recent publications include *Making Sense of Teaching* (with Sally Brown), *The School Mentor Handbook* and *Managing Student Teachers' Learning* (both with Hazel Hagger and Katharine Burn), *Strategies for Effective Teaching and Learning: Teachers' and Pupils' Perspectives* (with Paul Cooper) and *Developing Competent Teachers* (co-edited with David Hustler, David Fulton Publishers).

George Mardle, Lecturer, Department of Education, University of Keele, has been responsible for the further education elements of the PGCE course and currently supervises MA and PhD students in policy development and further education.

Trisha Maynard is a lecturer in the Department of Education, University of Wales, Swansea. For the past four years she has undertaken research into the role of the mentor in initial teacher education and is co-author (with John Furlong) of *Mentoring Student Teachers: The Growth of Professional Knowledge* (Routledge).

Debbie Wall is a Research Associate in the School of Education, University of Leicester. She has been the researcher and evaluator on numerous projects including 'Action Planning in Teacher Training', 'The Enterprise in Higher Education Initiative' and currently, 'Mentoring for Pre-clinical Medical Students'.

John West-Burnham is Professor of Education Management at Humberside University and was previously Director of the Distance Learning Programme, Educational Management Development Unit, University of Leicester. He is the author of *Managing Quality in Schools* (Longman).

CHAPTER ONE

Introduction

Donald McIntyre and Hazel Hagger

Among the many useful books that are being published about school-based teacher education, this one marks a new step forward. That it is a research-based book, telling us about realities of mentoring in schools, is important; but that alone is not what makes it so distinctive. This book is special not only because it is based on research but also because that research has in large measure been commissioned and/or conducted by school-based teacher educators themselves. It is true that the book has been written by people working in universities: they too were actively involved in the research and indeed did much of the planning and co-ordination of it. But, in that people working in schools themselves conducted much of the research, or determined what the research would be about, we claim that this book reflects a significant step forward towards genuine partnership between schools and universities in initial teacher education. That people in schools are doing half or more of the work of initial teacher education does not necessarily imply partnership; but when people in schools play an equal part in deciding what questions need to be asked and in determining the answers to those questions, we shall know that we have real partnerships.

Much of the credit for that distinctive characteristic of this book must go not to the authors but to the Esmée Fairbairn Charitable Trust which proposed and supported this programme of research. In the autumn of 1992, the Trust contacted six university departments of education (UDEs) – Keele, Leicester, Manchester Metropolitan, Oxford, Sussex and Swansea – inviting them to bid for funds to support a research and development initiative on mentoring. The Trust made it clear that the kind of initiative it sought would involve:

- active participation of school staff working in partnership with the universities

- research aimed at developing the quality of mentoring and at confronting problems which schools faced in the provision of good mentoring
- arrangements for the sharing of problems and of expertise among mentors at local and national levels.

It was in our view to the credit of the UDEs that they decided to collaborate rather than to compete, and to make a joint proposal to the Trust. The Trust's guidelines were found useful in shaping the proposed project and did not impose any unwelcome constraints. The joint proposal was based on a common framework within which the six UDEs would pursue distinctive but complementary research concerns. Three overarching themes were proposed:

Learning the new roles for school-focused teacher education

The central role is that of the mentor: research and development might be concerned with mentors' knowledge, their problem-solving, the effectiveness of learning through shared experience, with complementary roles such as those of professional tutors in schools and of HE staff.

Mentoring and the continuum of professional development

Mentoring in relation not only to initial teacher education (ITE) but also, for example, to induction, continuing staff development, and development in promoted roles: similarities, differences and interactions between phases.

Mentoring and institutional structures

Mentoring and the whole school context for teacher learning. Mentoring and school management structures, local management of schools (LMS), resourcing, etc. Implications of school-focused teacher education for HE facilities and departments of education.

At the local level, each UDE was to pursue its research in partnership with schools and would establish a Local Mentoring Forum for sharing expertise. At the national level, the initiative was to be centrally co-ordinated by a Project Management Group representing the Trust and the six UDEs. Three national seminars were to be held at six-monthly intervals, leading up to a national conference at which the work and achievements of the project would be publicised and disseminated.

These general proposals, and the specific proposals from each of the six universities, were accepted by the Esmée Fairbairn Charitable Trust and the project got under way during the summer of 1993. Most of the research data-gathering and the development activities were concentrated within the 1993–94 academic year. The national seminars were held in the autumn of 1993 and in the spring and autumn of 1994, and the final national conference took place at Keble College, Oxford in March 1995.

As intended, a great deal of fruitful sharing of insights and much constructive and vigorous debate has occurred through the distinctive provision for Local Mentoring Forums and for national seminars. We shall not however be attempting in this book to give accounts of these activities, nor of the Keble Conference. Instead, this book seeks to provide succinct reports of what we have learned from the six mutually complementary research projects; and, since versions of these reports formed the basis of seminars at the Keble Conference, we are able in our concluding chapter to take account of the discussions which the reports stimulated on that occasion.

The six research projects

Manchester Metropolitan

Because both teacher educators' own initiatives, and also government requirements, for a shift towards school-based initial teacher education (ITE) happened first in the secondary school sector, British ideas of mentoring in ITE have tended to be shaped in that context. The MMU project was therefore concerned with the distinctive issues that arise for mentoring in primary schools. With five mentors from diverse primary schools as key members of the research team, it explored the implications of primary school contexts, tasks, structures and cultures for the work of mentoring, and sought to identify sources of distinctiveness in primary school mentoring.

Swansea

Like that at MMU, the Swansea project was especially concerned with mentoring in primary schools. A mentor was seconded for a half day per week from each of five primary schools throughout 1993–94. These mentors worked with university tutors in planning and supervising student teachers' learning activities throughout the year. The particular focus of this work, and of the research based on it, was mentors' understanding of the substantive content of subject areas of the primary school curriculum, and their thinking about their own contribution as 'subject mentors' to student teachers' education in the content needed for primary school teaching.

Sussex

In keeping with the overall project's emphasis on mentor development, the Sussex research also was embedded in mentor development activities.

An explicit training programme for new mentors and professional tutors included days spent in two secondary schools working with their established ITE teams. In addition, mentor exchanges were set up to provide opportunities for inexperienced and experienced mentors in the same subject areas to visit each other in their respective schools. In the context of this training work, the experiences, thinking and practices of experienced mentors were made accessible not only to the beginning mentors but also to the researchers. The dominance of subject teaching in the work of secondary school mentoring led the researchers to focus particularly on the ways in which beginning teachers are inducted into school subject cultures.

Keele

This project was concerned with schools' arrangements for, and management of, mentoring. It involved case studies of twenty schools together with a questionnaire survey of one hundred mentors. The Keele team's attention had been drawn by the apparent wide variations among schools in their provision for student teachers. They aimed to investigate the validity of this impression, to explore the nature of the variations and to understand the sources of them. This then is a study of how whole schools take on and carry out responsibilities for initial teacher education, and of the ways in which the work of mentors relates to the organizational framework within which their work is set.

Oxford

The Oxford Internship Scheme is a school–university partnership scheme for secondary school ITE which was established in 1987, and thus offers a context within which some teachers have extensive experience of school-based ITE. Such teachers are well placed to identify important questions. The Oxford project therefore invited mentors and school-based professional tutors to submit proposals for suitable studies such as documenting existing good practice, investigating problems and trying out ideas for improved practice. A full-time researcher was appointed for one year to conduct the research under the direction of those proposing the investigations, and with the support of the university-based director of the project. Five such studies were proposed by the teachers and all of them were undertaken.

Leicester

The distinctive feature of the Leicester project has been its focus on the concept of mentoring in respect of three phases of professional development beyond ITE: newly qualified teachers, middle managers and headteachers. To what extent, they asked, does the notion and practice of mentoring differ across these phases? The views of mentors and protégés have been sought in relation to such issues as the appointment of mentors, the purposes and processes of mentoring, factors influencing the quality of mentor performance, and the implications of mentoring for whole school management structures and processes.

Some common themes

As already noted, the six UDEs planned that the individual projects would be shaped by a common framework and be mutually complementary. In retrospect, we believe that this has in practice been achieved, although in the course of the work the overarching themes have inevitably been modified, clarified and elaborated. In the concluding chapter we shall discuss thematically the problems that have been illuminated and the lessons which can be learned from the research findings of the six projects. At this point it may be helpful for us to identify the seven general themes in terms of which we shall discuss conclusions. We see these themes as being important for policy and practice and also as being dominant themes cutting across the reports of the different projects.

The concept of mentoring

It is not obvious why the term 'mentor' should have become so widely used in British education during the last ten years. It has been used in contexts other than schools, and also in North America, for rather longer, and it brings with it from these other contexts certain connotations which may or may not be helpful in the contexts with which we are here concerned. In relation to ITE in particular, one has to ask whether these connotations, for example of a very personal relationship and of informality and lack of structure, are helpful in thinking about the roles of school-based teacher educators.

To what extent are the different roles to which the term mentor has been attached in schools comparable? The Manchester Metropolitan project looks at mentoring in primary and secondary ITE contexts; the Swansea project introduces the new idea of 'subject mentoring' and explores the distinctive features of that kind of role; and the Leicester project examines the task of 'mentoring' at three different levels within school hierarchies, all of them concerned with the professional development of practising teachers. In so far as such diverse tasks are comparable, there may be great scope for mutual learning in terms of the elucidation of problems and the identification of good practice and what facilitates it. We have to be cautious, however, about assuming that these tasks *are* comparable, that for example the term 'mentor' can be sensibly used with the same meaning for subject learning as it is for learning about classroom practice, or for new headteachers as it is for newly qualified teachers. Is there a danger of being seduced by our terminology into assuming that very different needs can be effectively met through rather similar strategies?

The mentoring school

One particular way in which the term 'mentor' may possibly have misled us in relation to ITE is that its connotation of a very personal relationship may have led us to overemphasise the individual responsibility of a particular person as opposed to the institutional responsibility of the school. That is the central concern of the Keele report. In addition, two of the Oxford investigations indicate the importance, but also something of the difficulty, of ensuring that ITE in secondary schools is accepted as a responsibility of whole subject departments. Similarly at the primary level, the MMU project emphasizes the whole school culture but also the fact that not every teacher makes a good teacher educator. The Keele project examines the ramifications of engagement in ITE partnerships for school managements and for staff in general, and the considerable impact on ITE quality of whole-school policies and practices.

What then are the characteristics of a good 'mentoring school'? How many schools have these characteristics already, without deliberately developing them, because of their involvement in ITE? How realistic is it to expect whole schools to be so committed to ITE as to make it a significant element in their own development planning? Or is it possible that the quality of ITE depends on a small number of individual committed specialist mentors?

Partnership

The projects reported in this book are all focused on the work of mentors in schools. Nonetheless, all those concerned with ITE explicitly or implicitly raise questions about the terms of the schools' partnerships with higher education institutions (HEIs). The Keele project in particular raises questions about many different aspects of ITE programmes. Four main questions emerge in relation to every aspect of partnership programmes:

- How *clear* are the conditions of the partnership: what is expected of the partners in terms of what will be done when, and how, and in relation to what criteria of quality?
- What *division of labour* is seen as being appropriate between universities and schools, and as being realistic in terms of each institutions' capacity to make effective provision for different kinds of learning experiences?

- To what extent, and in what ways, is student-teachers' work in the two contexts *integrated*, so that what is done in the university is effectively used in school-based learning, and what is done in each context is effectively questioned in the other?
- What kinds of *constraints* limit the realisation in practice of theoretical conceptions of the kinds of partnership which should be operating between schools and universities?

Subject knowledge and beliefs

It appears that subject knowledge and beliefs are an especially difficult aspect of effective ITE partnerships. This is the primary focus of the Swansea and Sussex reports, although the issue takes rather different forms at primary and secondary stages. Among the questions which these two studies in particular help us to address are the following:

- In both primary and secondary contexts, what aspects of subject knowledge provide the most appropriate focus?
- To what extent can schools be expected to take responsibility for 'filling gaps' in student teachers' subject knowledge?
- In what ways can the university and the schools work together most effectively in preparing student teachers to think about their own and others' underlying beliefs and to enable them to see the influence of these beliefs on how the subject is taught?
- What parts should the university and the schools play in helping student teachers to develop 'pedagogical content knowledge'?
- What measures can be taken to ensure that student teachers are assessed fairly when they do not themselves subscribe to the distinctive subject cultures (or indeed anti-subject cultures) of particular departments or schools?

Resourcing and quality control

A recurring theme throughout the several reports (and indeed in other literature on mentoring, both in ITE and in other school contexts) is the shortage of time for mentors to do their work effectively. Often mentors sacrifice leisure time in order to meet the needs of their students. In these circumstances it is not surprising that there should be wide variations in provision across, and indeed within, schools. Equally unsurprising are the difficulties involved in the establishment of criteria and procedures to reduce such variation. Are the resources allocated to schools adequate? How can quality control procedures be effectively operated in partnerships of autonomous institutions? It seems rather unlikely that market forces will provide an acceptable answer.

Benefits for the schools

One possible resolution of the problem of adequate resourcing might be through a recognition of the non-material benefits that can come to schools through engagement in ITE. Again this is a recurring theme across several of the reports, and one explicitly studied in two of the Oxford investigations. What merits are there in claims about:

- benefits to pupils?
- opportunities for teachers to develop their own teaching?
- stimulus to collaboration among teachers?
- opportunities for the development of managerial and other transferable skills?

What conditions are necessary for such benefits to be realized? Are schools actively planning to realize these benefits? Should they be? Are universities providing the support which would be useful to help the schools realize such benefits?

Developing mentoring

As noted earlier, this final theme was one which the Esmée Fairbairn Charitable Trust wisely emphasised in initiating and supporting the research reported here. Given that the tasks of mentoring in schools, for ITE and other purposes, are still new and relatively undeveloped, how best can effective mentoring strategies be developed and refined? The work reported in this book reflects a variety of ways in which mentors have been engaged in exploring the boundaries or the problems of their own work – as action researchers, as experts whose thinking is studied, and as commissioners of research. What conditions and support are necessary to enable mentors to develop the confidence and the expertise to shape and develop their own roles? That is perhaps the most fundamental question.

CHAPTER 2

Mentoring and Primary School Culture

Anne Campbell and Ian Kane

The research findings indicate that many aspects of primary school culture, while often producing the tensions discussed below, are of great importance to the development of effective mentoring. It is not enough to provide a collaborative ethos; support and leadership from the management of the school, skilled, reflective mentoring and precise useful feedback to students are all necessary ingredients. Willing classteachers who are able to negotiate appropriate contexts for student learning have a central role.

Context and methodology

The immediate context in the Didsbury School of Education for the original proposal to the Trust was Circular 9/92. The School of Education, in accordance with Government policy, was working with 120 partnership secondary schools in piloting transition towards school-based teacher training, involving an extensive mentor preparation programme. At the same time, experience of mentoring was being evaluated in the North West Consortium Articled Teachers Scheme, (see Campbell and Kane, 1993) with both secondary and primary routes, but mainly the latter. A first year BEd programme had evolving mentoring links with primary schools and with practitioners on the University's inservice programmes, notably the MA(Teaching). A Primary Associated Schools Project was already established in the BEd, while the primary PGCE was piloting not only mentoring in the supervision and assessment of teaching practice but a Collaborative Teaching Project as well. It was possible to cross refer this work to the School Of Education's New Teacher in School Project, (see Archer and Hogbin, 1990), which over three years had been evaluating the effectiveness of the BEd. Prior to Circular 9/92, the PGCE (Secondary) course had introduced 'Learning Contracts' (see Hustler *et al.*, 1995) for all students. The learning contracts provided a framework for students, mentors and tutors to review and set targets in relation to the acquisition of professional competencies. That framework was viewed as having considerable potential, drawing on experience with Compacts and Training Enterprise Councils. Thus, interest in mentoring had grown, much of it to do with initial teacher training, arguably to the neglect of newly qualified teacher (NQT) and other mentoring.

Rapid developments had occurred in mentoring for secondary school trainees yet regional experience suggested that, although there were some common mentoring issues across primary and secondary schools, there were also distinctive primary issues which required urgent attention. Nonetheless, work on secondary mentoring could not be ignored. The solution appeared to be to incorporate a comparative dimension and to seek to establish possible similarities and differences across different age-phases. However it was a deliberate choice in this project to focus on mentoring in the primary school.

The approach adopted involved case studies in five schools and was supported by action research within the schools. The aim was to investigate mentoring in the schools in order to provide a 'platform of understanding' (Kemmis, 1980) for future development of partnerships between schools and higher education. The research team consisted of five experienced mentors (from the schools) and five tutors.

Starting points: the schools and encounters with secondary mentoring

We provide here enough detail on each school for the reader to have some sense of the primary school worlds involved in the project and of the contrasting contexts. These brief descriptions are followed by extracts from the initial personal statements from the mentors. They also contain the questions which were in our mind as we involved these schools in the project. Not all the questions proved to be significant, as we progressively concentrated on cultural aspects.

School A

School A lies four miles north of the Manchester city centre. Most of the children are physically well cared for but many have emotional problems often stemming from the effects of unemployment, poverty and social and economic deprivation. The need for stable relationships between pupils and staff is self evident. Could a new transient population of student teachers spending longer in the school have a de-stabilising effect? Did the school already have enough to do without taking on an enhanced role in initial teacher training?

The mentor was the Deputy Head. The school had been involved in ITE research projects with the Manchester Metropolitan University for some years and both the Head and the Deputy were studying for higher degrees. Mentoring experience was extended by the involvement of the Head in the LEA pilot scheme for mentoring new heads.

The mentor:

> Last year, for the first time in my career, I acted as official mentor to two second year students, although I have been involved with newly qualified teachers and students many times over the years. Taking on the mantle of official mentor, I was interested in how the role would differ from any of my pre-conceived ideas, and how the role could be developed. Although not everyone may choose to develop or utilise their skills, with encouragement many staff can channel their abilities into mentoring.

School B

School B is a two form entry primary school (4–11). The catchment area is broad, ranging from large detached owner occupied properties through semi-detached and terraced housing to a large estate of council properties.

The percentage of ethnic minority families with origins across the world has increased from about 10% to nearly 30% in the last five years. Many children cannot speak or understand any English on entry to school, and there has been a lack of training for established staff. Did this school, with a pupil population so demonstrably a cross-section, constitute an excellent testing ground for mentoring in practice?

School B had had connections with the MMU for many years. The Deputy Head was chosen to participate in the mentoring project. She too was registered for her MEd at Didsbury, her research focusing around the theme of the impact of mentoring students on the school as a whole.

The mentor:

> I have been involved with the mentoring of students, probationary teachers, NQTs, and new staff over a number of years, although the title 'mentor' has only recently been introduced. I have always felt that a sense of personal value accompanies such a role, as the schools involved have given the subject a high profile, the success of the mentee being a reflection of the school's commitment to professionalism and professional development. The time allocated by the school specifically for the purposes of mentoring has not, however, matched those statements of high priority. Mentoring in my experience, is an aspect of the job description tagged on at the end with no in-built provision. Any time in terms of supply cover has had to be fought for, and always brought with it a sense of guilt that someone else or another aspect of school life has had to suffer because of it.

School C

School C is a junior school, a light modern building in a leafy suburb in an LEA which still retains the eleven-plus, and where success in gaining entry to independent schools is a significant parental aspiration. Parental involvement is high; meetings and school activities are well attended. The governing body is active, professional and committed.

How would an increased involvement in initial teacher-training be seen by parents, traditionally very interested in eleven-plus success or other forms of competitive entry to secondary education? How would an informed, active and powerful governing body respond? What pressures would be felt from an articulate, assertive set of parents?

The school had worked with MMU on a number of schemes designed to explore the potential of more school-based initial training. The scheme of which there was most experience was the Collaborative Teaching Project in the PGCE, a three-way project involving teachers, tutors and students in negotiated topics. As both Deputy Head and Acting Head, the Esmée team mentor had accepted responsibility for students on placement for several years.

The mentor:

> I have always been a teacher who has welcomed the opportunity to work with students. I have seen this work as part of my professional development, and was excited, although rather apprehensive, to be asked to act as mentor for a project in 1993. I was already aware of the discussions in educational circles of the role of mentor in school-based initial teacher training. What, I asked myself, was a mentor? I looked up the word in a dictionary – 'an experienced and trusted adviser'. I could accept that I was an experienced teacher with a wealth of expertise about primary school children. I felt that the two key words for me were 'trusted adviser'.

School D

School D has inner city characteristics although the two form entry infant school is at the suburban fringe. It has the largest playground of any school in the authority but virtually no grass; matching this is the second smallest floor area so that 'incomers' make a difference. Governors regularly receive reports on ITE from the headteacher. The mentor herself has been in school for 17 years. She would say without hesitation that the strength of the school is that it is, was and continues to be a very cohesive unit where staff support each other and work closely together on any and all initiatives. The Head's view at the outset was that involvement in mentoring was useful and supportive as a staff development exercise.

Might an increased number of 'incomers' disturb the valued harmony? What would mentoring feel like as staffing pressures began to bite? Was this a good proving ground for a whole school approach?

The mentor:

> I was very happy to agree to be a mentor because I would hope that one of my strengths is that I am always open to new ideas. I would quite readily admit that I have concerns. They are to do with my own ability to have discussions with the students and write reports in the way they were used to having them from their tutors in the past. I was not worried about the classroom observation aspect because I was now quite used to involvement in all the classes throughout the school as that was the greatest part of my role during that school year. I was not concerned about the unusual situation of being in another teacher's room observing what was happening but I hoped that they would not feel embarrassed or inhibited by it.

School E

This inner-city junior school reflects the ethnic characteristics of the local community. Though housing thirty nationalities, the majority of children are from families originally from Pakistan. It is in many ways mono-cultural. Would differences in attitude and approach by parents and governors be visible, by contrast with the other schools?

The school has various close connections with MMU. This mentor, though not in this case a Deputy Head had, even so, some experience as an acting deputy. He was, moreover, an allowance holder with a designated responsibility for mentoring NQTs. He had been on several training courses and was interested in making connections between NQT mentoring and evolving partnership schemes. Like some others, he was registered on an MMU Masters degree, with Mentoring Developments as a dissertation theme. The school had regularly taken students on conventional lines but was interested to explore new thinking.

The mentor:

> Mentoring is very difficult. It seems to me that mentors need to possess the following qualities: an ability to empathize with beginning teachers; an ability to listen to their concerns and to discuss these concerns in a constructive way; an ability to observe their teaching in order to provide feedback which the NQT might find useful; an ability to explain the various policies and practices of the school, and how these function in theory and in reality.

Looking at secondary schools

The primary school teachers in the research team were well-experienced in mentoring from the outset. They had worked with student teachers over several years and each had had a role in one or other of the various MMU pilot schemes. It seemed appropriate to begin by exposing them to the fast developing work of preparing mentors for new secondary courses – which began in September 1994 – and then inviting them to draw on their mentoring experience and primary backgrounds to look for similarities and differences, for lessons for primary schools or alternatively for awful warnings.

Accordingly they attended one of a series of full day conferences for secondary 'central mentors', i.e. the mentor with single central responsibility for ITE in 120 partnership secondary schools. The conference was the first of the 1993–94 academic year. Team members shared in plenary sessions, sat in on groups and shared thoughts informally over lunch and other breaks. Subsequently they visited a secondary school with a high level of involvement and took part in a seminar conducted by the central mentor. A later visit to another school studied in more detail the impact of the changes on the school, observing these at first hand through discussions with a range of staff and students. Finally each team member was paired with a secondary mentor at a nearby school for further observation and discussion. They recorded their thoughts and were systematically de-briefed.

'Similarities' identified were much what one might have expected – commitment in principle to the concept of school-based training; worries about communications; concerns over funding; recognition that whatever the funding, old fashioned goodwill would contribute to topping up the student entitlement and would lead to variability of experience; the need for quality time to do the job properly; the usefulness of clusters as an organisational concept; fear of isolation, if HE withdrew or was excluded from teacher training; the threat of the de-professionalisation of teaching as a consequence; recognition that students needed a higher education base for tutor and peer support; the importance of a 'whole school' approach; the consistent involvement of senior staff as mentors rather than the use of teachers closer to the student teachers in age and experience (possibly now a changing trend); uncertainty about roles and particularly about having to assume an assessment role.

Much of that was predictable. Arguably more revealing were the areas of difference that this team of interested, knowledgeable, experienced primary mentors noted:

- the existence of non-contact time, with much more flexibility available in secondary schools,
- size: the larger the school, the greater the range of experience and expertise accessible to student teachers,
- size: the inability of primary schools to absorb students in anything like the numbers which secondary schools were accommodating; to quote directly, 'There's not enough chairs and not enough loos',
- the fact that secondary classes were subject based, while primary classes were whole curriculum based, which carried implications for mentoring and mentor knowledge; in particular, how *subject expertise* might be mentored in primary schools, (and see below)

- a belief that the twin roles of central mentor and subject mentor evolving in secondary schools did not carry a matching parallel in primary schools, where class teachers would seem to have the key role throughout,
- a recognition that class teacher mentors would nonetheless require preparation for their roles, however defined, no less than, but clearly *different* from, secondary central or subject mentors,
- the relative absence of significant numbers of NQTs in primary schools which ruled out the sharing of certain sorts of induction provision, generating more feeling of isolation by student teachers from peers, or near peers,
- simply finding potential mentors; while within most secondary departments there could normally be found one person at least to act as a mentor, primary school staffing seemed far more volatile,
- an apprehension that the much larger number of primary schools likely to be involved in ITE might well dilute even more the involvement of university tutors weakening still further school-university links, when the need for continuing support was predicted to be greater in primary schools. The HE tutor as 'subject expert' appeared to be a clear continuing role, conceptually, but was as yet no part of the thinking which lay behind evolving primary partnerships. (At the National Seminar it was interesting to discover that other project members were observing this same phenomenon.),
- the process of the identification of mentors appeared to be more the subject of negotiation and consultation in secondary schools, involving several levels of management, while in primary schools it was seen as primarily the decision of the headteacher, after more limited consultation,
- the impact of ITE would be even more under the microscope in a primary school with parental interest more likely to manifest itself, carrying with it consequent governing body interest,
- personal tensions would be magnified in primary schools, both student–class relationships and student–class teacher relationships, more than in situations in which student teachers ranged across a school and between classes,
- on the other hand, primary school mentoring could be more natural: there was less need for teachers, including 'strange' teachers, to explain their presence in the classroom than seemed to be the case in secondary schools.

Of particular interest was whether the conceptualisations of mentoring and mentoring practices within the primary school had any features which distinguished these conceptualisations and practices from mentoring in the secondary school context. Our initial speculation (and we have seen no reason to change this view) was that any divide between primary and secondary mentoring might have more to do with differences in primary and secondary cultures, than with features such as size, or organisational structuring, *per se*.

Some examples illustrate this. Arguably it was unsurprising that the class teacher role should be seen as more important than the five mentors thought it was in secondary schools. However, had they had detailed access to the ways in which secondary mentoring subsequently evolved, they might have seen a slow but progressive shift towards an increasing emphasis on that role too. On the other hand, they did not reject the concept of 'overarching' mentor as being a necessary one, although the explanation for this lies possibly in the fact that that is the role they were discharging, and given the stage of development of school based training, discharging successfully and crucially. A recommendation for self-immolation is a rare phenomenon in education. But what are we to make of the ambiguous response to subject mentoring? If, as indicated, it is acknowledged that the class teacher is a significant player, for primary mentors the explanation for this appeared to lie principally in that person's closeness to the student; it did not seem to have much to do with that person's subject knowledge. Consequently although the mentors shrewdly perceived that there was a gap to be filled and an unanswered question 'Who will provide the necessary subject knowledge for mentors and students?', they did not make any challenge to the widely held belief that the primary school teacher's role is a generalist one. They did not, for example, raise the question of what part a subject co-ordinator, or post-Dearing subject 'manager', might play. This is unsurprising. 'Wise men' and others have come and gone but the introduction of secondary style subject specialism, even into Key Stage 2 teaching, seems little nearer than it was twenty years ago. The belief in the virtue of the generalist teacher model, albeit with some, usually annually negotiable, specialist responsibility dominates primary school culture.

Another issue raised which re-appears later is that of 'outsiders' – the presence of people around the school and in the classrooms: parents, helpers, visitors. Arguably this is partly a matter of visibility – the smaller the space, the more others are noticeable – but partly it may well be cultural. There is not so much a willingness to have other adults around primary schools as a traditional acceptance that they will be around – aided by an ease of access not available to security conscious secondary schools. To some extent, too, primary schools value extra hands because of the relief they give when non-contact time is at a premium – another issue which led our mentors to look at the question of time for mentoring in a different way.

On the whole, therefore, we think our mentors correctly observed the differences between primary and secondary schools. Although there were differences relating to size and organisation, many of the differences were culturally determined. Perhaps most significantly, the way mentors looked at the subject knowledge question and the conclusion they arrived at – which we would not necessarily share – was heavily influenced by primary school culture.

It is acknowledged that the work done in the project has been with a small sample of primary schools, all with experience of mentoring, but which vary considerably in the nature and roots of their mentoring experience and practice. Certainly part of our work has been to contextualise mentoring vis-a-vis each of the settings, so that we would be increasingly able to think about some of the features shared across the participating primary schools. The use of secondary schools as a laboratory was a research tool operating as a device through which we might sharpen up some understandings concerning mentoring in the primary context and find possible ways into the distinctive features of primary mentoring.

Our interest in cultural issues had been manifested in our initial approach to the research process which is why we began by focusing on the participants' experience and the meanings they attached to mentoring and why each mentor kept a journal; why too mentors and tutors wrote a short personal statement at the outset, outlining their experience and interest. Each individual's research journal provided starting points. Through a reviewing process, we revisited, developed and reformulated those starting points. The secondary contacts programme described above was the beginning.

Stakeholders' views

The culture of the five primary schools was shaped and influenced by the stakeholders in the venture – those who had a vested interest in the conduct and development of school-based teacher education. For the purposes of this section it is proposed to illustrate the attitudes, behaviours and social norms evolving in schools by presenting the views of headteachers, parents, governors, mentors and pupils and thereby to gain insight into major influences on schools in the project.

Headteachers

The head teachers of the five schools were each interviewed during February and March 1994. The following draws on these interviews and on the headteacher questionnaire. (One hundred questionnaires were completed at the Regional Dissemination Conference in November 1994.)

None gave uncritical support to the move to more school-based teacher training. All five saw the partnership with higher education as very important: 'We greatly value the MMU input and cannot envisage going off alone; it would not be viable.' Whilst most primary heads at the Regional Conference agreed with this statement, 50% of secondary heads did not. Arguably, this is more a sign of growing confidence in the role than a declaration of intent.

Two heads who were interviewed felt strongly that it was *not* their job to train teachers, and all five put the teaching of children before anything: 'Our priority is the children, yours is the students.' Approximately 88% of primary heads from the larger group agreed with this statement and 91% of secondary headteachers. Two project heads saw the move to school-based training as a political imposition by the Government and an attempt to deprofessionalise the teaching force. They explicitly stated that, while feeling they did have something to offer to students, they preferred the 'old' system, where Higher Education was in charge and tutors supervised the students. Their views, in our experience, are widespread and are indicative of the conflicts in priorities between teaching children and teaching students experienced by many schools.

Most head teachers had major concerns regarding the funding and did not think, on the evidence available, that the move to school-based training was likely to be properly resourced. Four of the five schools used the non-class teaching deputy as the mentor, the fifth used an allowance holder with responsibilities for mentoring newly qualified teachers. This practice of using a non-class teacher as mentor significantly reduces the need for supply cover and leaves some schools in the situation of viewing the money allocated by Higher Education as 'an extra perk'. One head felt that students could be disadvantaged and be 'like second class citizens and treated like ancillaries', if the funding remained inadequate. It was apparent to all five that mentors and class teachers gave much more time than that which was officially funded. Unsurprisingly the larger group of heads, consulted in November, endorsed the view that funding levels were inadequate.

Time was also a major concern. Schools acknowledged that they could not provide enough time 'for debating key education issues or for sitting around in groups talking'. One speculated that that was precisely what the Government wanted to eradicate from teacher education anyway. Time for mentoring was also viewed as problematic, mentors giving up their lunchtimes and much of their own time after school to support students. This point was reiterated strongly by mentors after their visits to secondary schools.

Further exposure to school life was seen as one of the more positive aspects of more time in school – though there was some recognition that more school-based time for students could increase the likelihood of exhaustion and of too high expectations of them on the part of teachers. This pressure is the same as that experienced by many Articled Teachers, (see Campbell and Kane, 1993) – namely a tendency to view students as 'real teachers'. Resultant staff development from involvement in mentoring, the development of whole-school approaches and closer partnerships with Higher Education were recognised and welcomed. Interpersonal skills, management skills and improved co-ordination and organisational abilities were pinpointed as areas of development.

Some of the dangers identified were focused around the issue of student dependency. The tensions apparent in the support–assessment continuum implicit, indeed sometimes explicit, in the role of mentor, caused difficulties related to lack of objectivity in assessing students. 'A mentor has a position of power which can be abused' and 'Without the mentor and class teacher support she would have failed her practice, without a doubt. That begs the question of whether we should offer so much support'. Students too can abuse the system. 'Students are manipulative – they want the best deal out of us, quite rightly – they manipulate us emotionally.' Our research shows there to be a split in primary and secondary headteacher views about student dependency on mentors, the primary schools being less concerned about dependency and accepting a heavy support role as a necessary part of development. Despite headteachers stated views that it is a straightforward task to fail students who are being strongly supported by the school, our observations and experience indicate that there are numerous occasions when there is a great deal of pressure on schools and mentors not to fail students. The difficulties in learning to move along the continuum of support and assessment, and of selecting appropriate strategies for supervision, are not acknowledged by headteachers, reflecting the need to explore further understandings of mentoring.

Similarly, the issue of accommodating able students in a school staffed by 'average' teachers was raised by three head teachers, indicating the need for development in mentoring approaches and strategies.

There were concerns about 'student entitlement'. How could it be ensured that all students had a fair chance when school contexts varied so much? Were there dangers of 'cloning' students to teach in particular types of schools? Did the ethos of certain schools, or the relationships in them, disadvantage students? The majority of the larger group of heads consulted was not concerned that entitlement was difficult to ensure, an arguably complacent position given the variety of contexts and environments experienced by students in the North West.

Parents and governors

Two members of the team, deputy heads and mentors in contrasting schools, (C and D), investigated the views of parents and governors about school-based training and partnerships with higher education.

In summary, the investigation suggested that parents have no clear understanding of the work of students in school, their role being seen mainly as an 'extra pair of hands'. They felt that the mentoring role had positive aspects, but were concerned about the extra work load upon already very busy class teachers. Parents agreed that 'hands on' experience for the students must be valuable and felt that when students were good and could take over the class teacher's role competently, then the class teacher would have valuable time for particular children or groups who needed extra help. Generally they felt a monetary incentive was important but might not benefit the whole school and did not understand that previously schools had not been paid to receive students. Some parents had quite a high awareness of the proposals for change.

Issues of concern included a belief that the higher education establishment should provide a theoretical background while the school gave practical experience and there was a great sense of unease about the shift from one to the other and worry that some students might not have such good experiences Parents were sceptical that the national change was other than a cost cutting exercise, where schools would not gain from any reduction of funding to Higher Education. They anticipated a greater demand on schools' resources and significant impact from students. They were generally unsure about anything, even in-service training, which took the class teacher away from the classroom and found it hard to see beyond the present to long-term issues which did not affect their children. They expressed themselves as tired of new-fangled ideas in education, considered a student to be second best, and wanted only the best for their children. Accordingly they favoured pilot schemes and felt the new initiatives should be carefully monitored. They re-iterated that a teacher's job was first and foremost to teach pupils, and saw the demands of ITE as unfair on teachers.

The above views serve to illustrate how much still needs to be done in working with parents and carers to develop better understanding and key roles in the education of their children. Governors' views were broadly similar, but occasionally subtly different.

Governors in general felt that as with any other new initiative they should be consulted. They felt the implications for the school could be enormous, and questioned whether they as governors would be involved in drawing up a policy. They were clear that the main function of the school was to teach pupils; they acknowledged the students' need to be given the opportunity to practise in schools but questioned whether it was the school's job to train teachers. Governors felt that if changes went ahead then they would have to be adequately resourced, and were worried about how they might respond to vociferous well-educated parents with definite views on most educational matters. There was concern that school resources might be used for ITE rather than the children. External assessments such as OFSTED raised particular issues and worries. Governors would expect a clear idea of the roles and responsibilities expected of the school before entering into any partnership. Uncertainty about entering into any contract with universities was expressed and governors feared that they might be dragged unwillingly into student or teacher appeals.

The priority of parents and governors is very clearly the education of the children by the most experienced and suitable teachers. What is interesting is the headteachers' views of parents and governors as evidenced in the questionnaire responses from the November 1994 Conference. While agreeing mostly (85% of primary headteachers and 81% of secondary headteachers) that governors should be fully consulted about partnership arrangements there was no such conviction that parents should (61% of primary heads and 51% of secondary heads agreed.) Seventy per cent of the secondary headteachers agreed that most parents were anxious about their children being taught for long periods by students, indicating a reflection of the pressure of assessment and examination requirements in secondary schools. Only 55% of primary headteachers envisaged parental anxiety. This possibly reflects the fact that additional personnel in the shape of parents, students, support teachers and other professionals are commoner in primary schools.

A sense of uncertainty and tentativeness emerges from discussions with parents and governors which demonstrates the precarious, and at times difficult, situations schools find themselves in today when parents are influenced by league tables and intensive media coverage. It is understandable that schools may be somewhat reticent in involving parents in discussions about partnership, but if school-based teacher education is to flourish, parents' and governors' support is crucial to the development of a culture which facilitates partnership in its widest sense.

Mentors

All mentors in the project supported the principle that while there should be more time in school for students in initial training, totally, or predominantly, primary school-based training was neither realistic nor desirable. There was anxiety about whether schools could offer students what they needed. Mentors valued tutors' contributions and acknowledged 'the wide experience of other schools which tutors have' and the 'high quality training – not just the subject matter but the processes of thinking and analysing which university staff encouraged in their students'.

Funding was generally viewed as important. They were divided over whether payment should be made to the mentor alone or to the school for resources and whole-school involvement. This tension with regard to funding is also apparent in other schemes: the Articled Teacher Scheme (Campbell and Kane, 1993), and partnership arrangements with secondary schools. It links closely with later discussion concerning the role of class teachers and whole-school mentoring. Mentors agreed that current funding arrangements were inadequate, given the cost of, and increasing need for, supply cover.

Mentors consistently acknowledged pressures experienced in their dual roles as mentor to students and teachers of children: 'This year I am class-based and I only get supply cover when I mentor'; 'It feels as if you are pulled in twenty-four different directions'; 'There is a lot of disruption for children'. All worried about other staff missing their support due to their mentoring.

Four of the five mentors were deputy head-teachers with staff development and support responsibilities; they saw mentoring, even with supply cover, as intrusive. Not being class-based was not always the easy answer: 'It's easier to cover for one class teacher than some of the fourteen classes which I take during the week'. Meanwhile problems of continuity for children were raised by the use of supply cover. Most mentors preferred to have 'internal' rather than 'external' supply teachers in the interests of both staff and pupils. In the future organisation of resourcing and staffing of schools, 'built-in' supply cover will need to be planned and well-structured to provide quality of experience for teachers, students and pupils. This begs the question in times of shrinking budgets of whether, and to what extent, 'in house' supply can be sustained. These pressures become more acute in the climate of the primary school where a supportive and collaborative ethos leads to the expectation of 'on tap support'.

An impressive list of qualities, skills and attitudes for mentoring was identified by those mentors interviewed within the project, ranging from counselling and interpersonal skills to observational and listening skills (Campbell, 1994b). The overall picture of a mentor is of someone who both wears the good teacher mantle and has the interpersonal skills required as an effective manager of adults. There was widespread agreement among mentors that being a good teacher did not necessarily mean being a good mentor. This contrasts with 'All teachers become potential mentors' asserted by McCulloch and Locke (1994) in their description of partnership with primary schools, an issue which is discussed subsequently.

In highlighting good practice in mentoring, and in describing cultures facilitating mentoring, an interesting list of obstacles was identified by the five mentors. *Time* for mentoring was, by far, top of the list. All participants felt very strongly that lack of time was the major obstacle to good mentoring. Other major obstacles identified by mentors were:

- lack of non-contact time
- poor management and leadership of school
- lack of funding
- lack of confidentiality
- non-involvement of staff
- unrealistic expectations of students' abilities and experience
- inappropriate placement of students
- lack of information from the university
- low status of mentor

Several of these issues are considered further in the concluding section of this chapter.

Pupils' views

A small survey of pupils' views of having students was undertaken in one project school. Children in Years 5 and 6 were asked to comment on what they saw as the benefits and disadvantages of having students, the length of time they spent in school and the activities and teaching they provided.

Some surprising findings resulted from this survey, not least of which was the general view and opinion about the role of the university tutor. Not one child surveyed had a good word to say for this role. The impact of the tutor's presence on the children is exemplified below:

> I find it difficult to concentrate on my work when the tutor comes in because I feel as if she is watching me. I feel like I am in an exam and I can't move. It might be a good idea if the tutor actually sat watching the student from outside the classroom.

was at times stronger than the children's perceived impact of the tutor's presence on the student:

> X acted differently when his tutor came.

> X got a bit more serious when the tutor came in.

> Students laugh and talk when their tutor is not about.

> I don't think tutors should come in to school – it puts off students and children, it makes the student act different to impress their tutors.

Children were quick to spot an assessment situation. Have they perhaps been influenced somewhat by the recent emphasis in primary schools on SATs and teacher assessment procedures? Indeed one child went as far as to suggest the pupils should write a report on students in order to help them to improve.

On the whole, children viewed the youthfulness of students as a positive factor and welcomed their entertainment value:

I prefer them young so they still have some fun left in them.

You tend to do more exciting things … talk to them about the score in a football match.

Students were often seen to be more approachable and friendlier than teachers, aspects which often backfire on them if children 'take advantage'.

Some sobering thoughts were raised by children about the quality of the teaching and learning opportunities they experienced with students. Complaints were made about lack of learning in science – 'Only had copy writing', and the simplicity of the level of work demanded of them. Children were divided in their views about the value of activities provided by students, influenced by comparisons with the norms in the school, parents' attitudes and the prevailing school work ethic. These factors no doubt influenced pupils' views as to the number of students there should be in school and how often classes should experience them and possibly reflected parental attitudes. Pupils were concerned about the management of students in school, most indicating that shorter periods of time were more beneficial, and that games and fun activities were better done by students than teachers.

Happily, not many subscribed to the following sentiment 'It's a waste of time. All they (the students) do is the teachers' dirty work.'

In fact, most children appreciated the extra attention they received due to the presence of students, perhaps echoing the view often expressed by many teachers about students as 'an extra pair of hands'. This can never be more than a minimalist view however. There remains a lot of work to be done in schools to help everyone become more aware of the students as novice-teachers or learner-teachers and the need for an appropriate learning environment supported by pupils and staff.

Evident also is the idea that students are different from teachers, implying less value with regard to learning and more value in respect of fun. This provides an interesting insight into how children separate enjoyment and learning in their experience of school. Perhaps one of the challenges for school-based teacher education is to link the experience of learning with that of enjoyment in more pupils minds?

The culture of the mentoring school

Collaboration

It's the person that matters – the mentor – not the school. (Manchester headteacher)

Our investigation would not support this assertion. There has been a gradual realisation and recognition of the importance to mentoring of school ethos and of the attitudes of staff, parents and governors. The impact of the culture of the school, the norms of behaviour, accepted work practices, expectations of 'inhabitants' and visitors to the environment, and the language used in schools – all of these contributed to and shaped the mentoring experiences of teachers and students. From the outset the concept of a primary school specific culture has been a constant point of reference. In drawing together the threads of the Manchester investigation, it is perhaps useful to accept, as a framework for discussion, the notion of 'the mentoring school'. Insofar as it is described by the five schools involved it may illustrate the importance of school culture to mentoring and its concomitant tensions and dilemmas. In the words of another headteacher in the project,

> The style of the school is important – where it is collaborative, and consultation takes place with staff, ... it is part of the ethos of the school ... Mentoring needs to be not exclusive to certain people, not externally imposed, but collaborative.

Further illustration of features identified as important to school culture conducive to mentoring can be gleaned from one mentor's analysis,

> Positive attitudes to working in a team – isolation is seen as dangerous ... we *have* to co-operate and share ideas. If teachers don't share and co-operate they're likely to end up in an early grave ... we need a warm environment where openness, trust and honesty are apparent, where we 'live by the rules'. I certainly couldn't exist in a negative environment. I need a sense of a staff being together ... we have got to be open to criticism, able to accept critical comments, and in the end be able to work together ... The worst thing is complacency, we must adapt and change and develop.

In general all mentors in the project subscribed to a similar viewpoint, which gives us an insight into the changes in the last 20 years. The climate, post-National Curriculum implementation, is a long way from Lortie's (1975) findings about the individualistic and private nature of teachers' learning and professional development. However, caution is advised with regard to the often identified 'collaborative culture' of primary schools. According to Nias (1989) and Holly and Southworth (1989) there are direct links between collegiality and school improvement, but there are many lessons to be learned from the complex interpersonal relationships and networks existing in primary schools which indicate the difficulties inherent in whole school policies and practices. In our opinion, the surface features of collaboration were on show in all five schools, but without further in depth investigation it is difficult to provide any evidence of refinement of practice, through, for example, peer tutoring, joint planning and team teaching.

Mentors in this study would agree that their schools were at different stages of development with regard to working together but the evidence from the interviews suggests a high general awareness of issues and developing practice. Collaboration is not easy. According to Little (1990) the quality of the collaborative practices, especially teachers' ability to give clear, precise and constructive feedback about teaching, is crucial to the success of any whole school development. This quality of collaboration is characterised by Fullan (1991) as 'continuous learners in a community of interactive professionals', but there was little evidence of the value and impact of mentoring approaches and practices on staff in the project schools even though more general statements such as 'Mentoring has highlighted the need to be *professional* at all times' has defined a somewhat generalised concept of mentoring, e.g. 'A good mentoring school is where everyone mentors each other'.

It would nonetheless appear that notions of the 'mentoring school' need much further investigation and possible reconceptualisation, particularly with regard to the sometimes conflicting interests of the pre-service and inservice education of teachers. McCulloch and Locke (1994) provide some valuable insights into primary schools in partnership with higher education and the need for whole school involvement, yet their assertion that 'all teachers become potential mentors' could be somewhat idealistic if an assumption of quality underlies the statement. Mentors and headteachers in the Manchester project acknowledged that while favouring and promoting a whole school approach, 'Not all good classroom teachers have skills with adults, such as management and counselling. Mentoring is different from teaching children'. Similarly, 'If you let people volunteer to be mentors it could be difficult if someone unsuitable volunteers'. Our conclusion from this part of the investigation is that all teachers, however experienced in traditional supervision of students, have other skills to learn in terms of the strategies for mentoring in ITE.

But, though it may be true that, 'It's the person', a caring, sharing, collaborative style is not enough. It may be necessary, yet not sufficient, for effective mentoring. Organisation and management also appear significant.

Effective leadership (and management) of school and personnel which supports, plans and facilitates adequate non-contact time, and adequate funding; a school which observes confidentiality, has realistic expectations of students and which gives high status to mentors – all seem major conditions for successful mentoring. Substantial emphasis was given by the five project schools to 'good relationships and communication' and to having 'a school where the aims are clear, where the policies are seen in practice (the living proof) in classrooms'. Mentors felt these were important features of a 'good' mentoring school.

Access to teachers' craft knowledge

Specific issues relate to craft knowledge. McIntyre and Hagger (1993) have expressed reservations about students' ease of access to teachers' craft knowledge. The assumptions expressed by Boydell (1994) that mentoring within a wider cluster of schools will almost certainly be a powerful influence on students' professional development may well be unfounded given the lack of research in this area. The assumption that 'classroom experience automatically provides the most appropriate learning' or that 'more experience is better experience', may yet prove incorrect (Dunne and Harvard, 1993). There is in any case, an underlying problem in describing and making explicit craft knowledge. Mentors in the project were beginning to develop a language with which to talk about their craft knowledge but acknowledged the difficulties.

> Where do you start? What elements of the teacher's role can you leave until a later date before they are brought into focus? The nature of the job is that all elements of the role are on view and working in a complex and highly interdependent system. It is difficult to be selective and thus not overload the student at the start.

However, much discussion about mentoring drew heavily on as yet unsystematised, uncategorised prior practice. All schools in the study were involved in a range of types of mentoring, from peer mentoring for staff development, new headteacher mentoring, newly qualified teacher mentoring and initial teacher education mentoring. There is no doubt that schools had gained much expertise in mentoring processes which shaped and influenced the culture prevalent in the five schools, and could be near to what Kelly *et al.* (1992) describe as a mentoring school and somewhat akin to Pedlar's 'Learning Company' (Pedlar *et al.*, 1989) where individual members of staff are encouraged to learn and develop their potential. Featherstone and Smith (1992) found from their experiences of peer mentoring in a Learning Support Team that

> The growing climate of confidence provides an excellent base from which to develop still further the notion of collaborative mentoring to a point where it becomes embedded within the structures of the school to the benefit of staff at all levels.

But there are dangers in a generic skills model and in 'embeddedness'. Elliott (1994) warns that some students may find occupational cultures detrimental to their learning. Campbell and Kane (1993) and Jacques (1992) identified this area as one of conflict for Articled Teachers, who experienced pressure to conform to the host school norms and philosophy while being urged by their tutors in Higher Education to appraise critically what they saw in schools. Thus a tension arises for mentors between encouraging appraisal and reflection while socialising new teachers into the culture of the school. The difficulties of teachers' stimulating reflection in their students is a concern voiced by a growing number of researchers such as Dunne and Harvard (1993) and Little

(1990). Vigilance is required if we are to maintain a symbiotic theory-practice relationship in the education of novice teachers and help new teachers develop the ability to talk precisely about their teaching in their reflection and evaluation.

A parallel problem experienced by mentors, which relates to *their* ability to talk explicitly yet reflectively about *their* teaching, is that of how to extend the more able student or NQT. One mentor commented,

> If you've got good NQTs or students you should leave them alone – how can you improve someone who is doing really well?

Yet, lack of intervention can result in student teachers' 'hitting the plateau', as described by Maynard and Furlong (1993), from which it is difficult to move on. This is a phenomenon frequently noted by HMI in their recent round of inspection of Circular 9/92 provision. There are many areas of development for mentors and models of mentoring as McIntyre and Hagger (1993) point out. It is perhaps at the 'Developed Mentoring' level, where collaborative teaching and planning expertise is required in order to move students from 'the plateau', that ability to talk about craft knowledge becomes essential. The problems of accommodating able students in a school staffed by 'average' teachers were raised by three headteachers in the project schools, (Campbell 1994a).

Arguably we could be expecting too much of mentors and schools. If the culture in school does not engender critical appraisal and reflection, and if, as we believe, teachers themselves find reflection difficult, how can mentors stimulate reflection amongst students? There are many aspects of primary school culture which work against the development of critical reflection on practice: time and space in which to actually reflect are difficult to provide due to the lack of non-contact time and the pressure on teachers to be working in classrooms with children; the value of reflection is often diminished by the need to conform to the latest DfE initiative or ring-binder in the mad rush to innovate; the pressure by inhabitants to socialise new recruits into the existing culture and norms (despite an awareness of the dangers of cloning, mentors still referred to students as 'fitting in' at school); the collaborative ethos set up in many schools that encourages conformity rather than conflict, although this can be healthy when characterised by recognition of individual differences. There is some indication from the project that mentors currently engaging in Masters action research courses find it easier to promote reflection and evaluation. (Note: Three out of five mentors were registered Masters students at Manchester Metropolitan University during the lifetime of the project.)

Tensions in managing student teachers' learning

No discussion of the culture of a mentoring school would be complete, nor would the Project be properly reported on, if reference were not made to several of the tensions which were exposed. It is important to recognise that in the Manchester Project we have been using a concept of mentoring where the mentor is distinct from the class teacher. Yet an area to which mentors continually returned in discussion was the overlap with the class teacher's role. All mentors felt that it has been undervalued, needs resourcing and should be seen as an important part of the mentoring process in schools, thereby coming closer to the McCullough and Locke (1994) model. There seems at present to be conflict in the overlap between the class teacher's role and that of the mentor, one of whom was explicit, 'Basically they (class teachers) do the day-to-day running of the student and their programme'.

One of the ways in which the class teacher role is undervalued is by the absence of any non-contact time in which to talk, plan and negotiate with students. In the hard-pressed situation in which most primary schools find themselves, releasing the mentor is difficult enough but the opportunity for class teacher release on a regular basis was found to be non-existent. The management of mentoring and students' learning needs to be part of the agenda of the senior management team in school. Such findings are not unique to our case studies. A study by Collison (1994) evidences the lack of time to mentor students, accompanied by findings that mentors and class teachers are not taking up opportunities in primary classrooms to interact. Collison advises that,

> Teacher mentors need to take a fresh look at their classrooms to accommodate the idea that firstly, unlike other adults in the classroom the trainees are there to learn and thus require some contact.

There was a feeling amongst mentors in the project that they had to be careful not to 'tread on others' toes'. Most schools had well established management structures and the one mentor of the team who did not belong to the senior management team felt very aware of status,

> Being a mentor and not part of the senior management team does raise issues about involving other members of staff. Not being responsible for managing people does make it more difficult to solve problems.

However, being a mentor and a deputy head, as four mentors were, brought its own set of dilemmas. Staff expected the same level of support as before, and parents and governors expected the same level of 'visibility' within the school. Conflict of interest is apparent when mentors focus their attention predominantly on students. Balancing being a teacher and being a mentor is difficult especially when there is more than one student placed in a school, and the mentor combines full-time class teaching responsibilities and a managerial responsibility e.g. Deputy Headship. The role is barely sustainable if there is not full support from other members of staff, in particular head teachers and class teachers hosting students. In one of the schools, where the ethos was not explicitly collaborative nor peer supportive, the mentor was aware that students were fairly low down on the list of priorities. She also indicated that there would be a fair amount of resistance to including initial teacher training and mentoring of students in the School Development Plan as suggested by McCulloch and Locke (1994). Arguably, there are particular tensions for mentors who are teachers of young children. In some of the more socially challenging environments where stability of teachers and adults who work with children is a prime concern, using a supply teacher and introducing a student need to be planned carefully to minimise disruption.

Confidentiality was mentioned by mentors as important.

> If people tell you they don't want anything going back to the Head – you have to use your judgement, try to make clear boundaries, what has to be either left unsaid, confidential, or made known to certain people, for the good of the school. You have to manage the situation.

Mentors were aware of the delicacy of some situations and gave examples of the following challenges: a student being critical of a teacher; a teacher openly criticising another member of staff; a mentor developing an intimate relationship with his mentee. Establishing the parameters for professional behaviour becomes, in our opinion, part of the collaborative ethos in school if situations like these are to be defused.

Loyalty to colleagues, to school philosophies and policies can also be stretched to the limit by situations arising out of mentoring.

> One NQT wanted to change current practice. I felt I had to be loyal to school policy in the staff meeting and this caused a problem with my mentee who wanted me to support the change. (Often) I have felt compromised.

Clearly, being a mentor is not easy, with times when not only professional issues are difficult to handle.

> While I could help with professional problems, I didn't feel I could help with the personal ones; that's not part of my job description. If you become too close to your mentee it could become very difficult.

Age too has a bearing: 'It's easier to be in a position of authority when the mentee is younger than you'. Mentors feel a need to distance themselves.

> I've always maintained that a good mentor needs to be slightly detached. There are certain aspects, if you get too close, that are difficult to tackle. It was of considerable benefit and help to me that I was a little distanced from the situation and from the class teacher. I took on the role of objective friendly supporter, but gave challenges, tutorial support and observation in the classroom.

As with distance, so with power. Mentors felt some need for status and power in relation to staff. Perhaps more interestingly, and as also identified by McIntyre and Hagger (1993), the potential abuse of power particularly in relation to assessment arose.

> The concentration into the hands of one person of the power to guide and assess the development of an individual learner–teacher's practice brings obvious dangers of arbitrariness and idiosyncrasy.

Mentors in the project were aware of this danger and talked about strategies to avoid the cloning of students. Again, all mentors found it easier to assess their mentee if they maintained some distance. Class teachers seemed to have a closer relationship with the student, and to be less objective since they often had an investment of interest and time in the satisfactory progress of the mentee. Headteachers joined mentors in an awareness of the dangers and tensions relating to assessment.

> It would be easier to fail someone as an external examiner than as a person who'd supported a student or NQT through the pain barrier for six months.

One headteacher felt that there were a number of temptations:

> It is a bit incestuous. Do you judge the student one way because you know the teacher? There is a danger of exposing staff or protecting staff. Do I cover things up as a head because I don't want to publicise bad things about my school?

Evidently, mentors confront not only professional issues. Personal issues raise problems. As reported it was claimed that being distant helped objectivity. However, possibly because personal and professional problems blur together, there can be times when the mentor's distancing from personal issues leads the mentee to turn elsewhere. There was some evidence that mentees chose other people as 'hidden' mentors for a variety of reasons: for subject specific support; for support in their personal life; and for help with individual pupils. This re-inforces the need for a whole school approach and for the establishment of a culture which facilitates development of a variety of styles of mentoring.

The honesty reflected in these interviews (Campbell 1994a, b), provided insight into other delicate issues. There was talk of how being a partnership and mentoring school might raise a school's profile and reference to getting used to having the extra money and perhaps letting the LEA off the hook with regard to increases in formula funding. Kane (1994) discusses and documents how parents' and governors' views shaped and influenced schools' responses to Higher Education partnerships in this particular project, and the general conclusions have been outlined earlier in this chapter. His findings indicate that parents and governors do not normally feel favourably disposed to having trainee teachers in school and have some general anxieties about young teachers. One school's parents and governors were particularly concerned that their OFSTED report might be affected by the quality of student teaching and the quality of mentoring provided by the school.

Conclusions

There is a great deal of realism in primary schools. They do not, in general think they can go it alone nor that they have the expertise and knowledge to train teachers. Teachers interviewed felt they had not the time, the resources nor the expertise to educate fully the next generation of teachers. There is accumulating evidence from our research at Didsbury that joint supervision, collaboration and dialogue between teacher–mentors in school, and most crucially between higher education tutors and teachers, is an essential part of school-based training. There is a gradual realisation of the complexity of supervision, the need to be able to select appropriate strategies to suit the context, to enable students to go beyond the plateau, to be able to challenge student practice and thinking beyond the obvious classroom management focus. It has been our experience that mentors and tutors alike are centrally concerned with helping students to develop the critical faculties to appraise, evaluate, refine and improve their practice so as to enhance pupil learning. They also want to be able to share craft knowledge with other teachers to promote continuous professional development and collective professional understanding and responsibility.

It is our conclusion following our investigations, centred as they were, principally, on in-depth case studies – but moderated by a wider audience as described – that mentoring in primary schools is significantly different from mentoring in secondary schools. Much of the difference lies in cultural contrasts. We would propose that certain conditions are necessary for good mentoring. These include:

- inter-personal skills
- a collaborative ethos
- whole school awareness
- constructive management.

The necessary inter-personal skills are arguably generic, although there is an issue to do with subject mentoring, which is far more clear cut in secondary schools. Most primary schools would claim that they strive for a collaborative ethos while secondary schools prefer to stress teamwork. Whole school awareness is possibly easier to achieve, because of size, than in larger secondary schools, but there are important differences between whole school awareness, whole school support and whole school involvement which seem to us to involve different managerial approaches. We cannot from our investigations subscribe to the concept of 'every teacher is a mentor' as a way forward in primary schools. In any case, one of our conclusions is that constructive management – normally by the headteacher – is as significant a factor as any: the deployment of supply cover, support and advice, the clear definition of responsibilities, the management of time, the processes of consultation with governors and parents. All the examples cited fall within the purview of the headteacher and are necessary, if effective mentoring is to occur in a primary school.

However, our principal conclusion concerns an issue which clearly relates mentoring to the particular culture of primary schools: it is the belief that the class teacher has a central role to play. Irrespective of whether the headteacher or other senior member of staff assumes a more general responsibility for mentoring, the role of mentor to students in training sits most naturally on a class teacher. Not all have the necessary skills and qualities. Thus, the potential of a primary school for involvement in mentoring partnerships is defined first, by the number of class teachers able to assume the role and secondly by the bounds a school sets on the amount of involvement of this restricted number of teachers. This decision is likely to be determined by the attitudes of parents, governors, other staff and by the putative mentors themselves.

In summary, if progress towards partnership is to be made in primary schools:

- they will need substantial continuing support from higher education,
- their capacity to participate in partnerships will be more limited than in secondary models,
- the number of suitable class teachers able and willing to participate is the key determinant,
- such limited resources as exist should be directed to facilitate and support the maximum involvement of suitable class teachers.

CHAPTER 3

Mentoring Subject Knowledge in the Primary School

Trisha Maynard

Introduction

In recent years, a succession of government circulars (DES 1984, 1989; DfE 1992, 1993) has ensured that not only will the vast majority of initial teacher education courses take place in partnerships with schools, but that the curriculum for these courses will be defined by the government as a series of competences on which students will focus for the whole of their training. By 1994, when courses must be explicitly designed to serve 'the Government's policy objectives for schools' (DfE: 1993) the 'right' of government to determine the structure, organisation and content of initial teacher education appears to have been established (Furlong and Maynard 1995).

Within this decade it is the voices of the New Right, and others close to the government (Alexander, Rose and Woodhead 1992), which appear to have most greatly influenced government thinking about teacher education and the content of reforms. The view of the New Right, represented by writers such as Sheila Lawlor, (1990) and Anthony O'Hear, (1986), is that the primary task for teachers is to induct the next generation of children into proven and worthwhile forms of knowledge. All that is essentially required in order to become a good teacher is a 'sound knowledge and love of the subject one is teaching' (O'Hear, 1986:16).

Others close to the government, citing 'downward trends' in pupil achievement and the acute shortage of subject expertise in primary schools (Alexander *et al.*, 1992), directly question the appropriateness and effectiveness of the child-centred ideology. This ideology – believed to be an important aspect of the culture of the post-Plowden primary school – is often characterised by slogans such as 'we teach children not subjects' and is associated with 'progressive' teaching methods (Alexander, 1984). Alexander, Rose and Woodhead and other writers belonging to the New Right maintain that it is the 'highly questionable dogma' of the child-centred ideology that unnecessarily complicates primary teaching and obstructs and impedes a focus on subject knowledge.

For the government, one way of attempting to bring about a more subject-centred approach to primary teaching is through reforms of Initial Teacher Training(ITT). In the recent Circular 14/93 (DfE 1993) the first three stated priorities for primary ITT centre on improving teachers' knowledge of subjects relevant to the curriculum in primary schools – particularly in the core areas of English, mathematics and science. But what is of particular interest in this Circular is not so much that teacher training courses are required to include a minimum of 150 hours of 'directed time' for the teaching of each of these core areas, but that 'directed time' may be spent either in schools or in higher education institutions (HEIs). Indeed, it is advocated that schools play a greater part in student teachers' curriculum and subject studies.

This recommendation means that from September 1996 when this Circular comes into force, it is likely that student teachers will spend some time focusing specifically on 'subject knowledge'. It is also likely that it will be teachers rather than HEI tutors who will be responsible for mentoring aspects of subject knowledge of the students on placement in their schools. It is this – mentoring subject knowledge in the primary school – that became the focus of our research at the University of Wales Swansea. It was not our intention that this project would result in a specific product: we were not, for example, aiming to produce a pack of materials to support teachers in undertaking this work. Rather, this project was seen as an opportunity to make an initial exploration of the implications and consequences of the process of mentoring subject knowledge.

Three questions guided our research:

1 What aspects of subject knowledge might be mentored in schools?

2 What are the possibilities, demands and constraints of subject mentoring?

3 What are the implications for schools and HEIs?

These questions will be addressed specifically in the conclusion. The chapter itself is divided into four sections that represent those issues we considered most relevant to our research: 'ways of working', 'thinking about subject knowledge', 'difficulties and demands' and 'teachers' attitudes towards subject mentoring'.

Ways of working

Initially, local schools were invited to bid for inclusion in our project, nominating a teacher who would take on specific responsibility for working with students. The five schools eventually invited to participate were chosen in part because of their stated enthusiasm and commitment to developing a whole school approach towards mentoring. We were also keen to recruit teachers who had a range of teaching experience in different settings. Of the five nominated teachers, three had extensive experience in both early years and upper primary classes, one teacher's experience was predominantly in the upper primary age range and the other in early years teaching. Their schools encompassed an urban junior, a semi-rural primary, an urban primary and two small primary schools – one urban and one Welsh valley with only three teaching members of staff. We had deliberately set out to include two small schools in our research in order to explore the possibilities of mentoring subject knowledge within the many small schools in Wales. Schools were given a grant of £2,000 for the release of the nominated teacher for the equivalent of half a day per week throughout the school year.

The teachers were asked to work with students in new ways. In the past they had worked as supervisory teachers: during students' serial practice in the Autumn term and on the extended block teaching experiences in the Spring and Summer terms, they had informally guided students' development in ways that made sense to them personally. As part of this project, teachers were required not only to develop their knowledge and skills as class mentors, but also to become the designated senior mentor – taking responsibility for planning and organising students' time within their schools. In the Autumn term, in order to support their development in this respect, the mentors used their release time to work with student teachers, with university tutors and with their teaching colleagues. They also attended an especially designed award bearing course which focused on the knowledge, skills and demands of becoming a class mentor and a senior mentor.

But our particular interest was in the process of mentoring subject knowledge in the primary school. One section of the course therefore involved them in designing and implementing their own action research projects which were to be centred on mentoring an aspect of subject knowledge with the student or students in their school. Although mentors were able to examine the content of students' college-based studies within their chosen subject area, they did not plan activities in collaboration with subject tutors from the university Department of Education. Rather, mentors took full responsibility for devising and implementing these activities. This, we felt, gave teachers more control over their projects and allowed us greater opportunities to explore their ways of thinking about the subject-matter content.

To facilitate the action research projects, the mentors, together with the author acting as researcher, formed an action research team. This team met every two to three weeks in the Spring and Summer terms and group discussions were recorded, transcribed and analysed (approximately twelve hours of recordings). Mentors were also interviewed individually and recordings of these interviews were transcribed and analysed (approximately seven and a half hours of recordings.) In addition, the researcher took on the role of tutor for students in two of the participating schools and spent a day in each of these schools for every week of the students' two block-teaching practices (twelve weeks). Field notes were made of observations and discussions with students, senior mentors and other teachers.

Mentors chose to focus their action research projects on four subject areas: English (reading and handwriting); mathematics (oracy in mathematics); geography (the use of the environment); and art (print making). The basic structure of the activities followed a simple pattern. Initially there was some kind of input such as reading, instruction on techniques and discussion followed by a task and finally, a feedback session where mentors tried to help students analyse, evaluate and understand the significance and implications of their task.

The underlying purposes of activities, and the role mentors assumed in the process of mentoring subject knowledge, varied. Some activities focused on challenging students' preconceptions or misconceptions, such as 'that text is the sole or most important factor in reading'. One mentor devised a series of activities which aimed to make the learning directly 'visible' to students. Students were asked to observe four different tasks given to pupils and evaluate how far each of these promoted discussion and learning. Some activities were intended to 'sensitise' students – for example, to the difficulties pupils had with handwriting – and yet others focused on instructing students, for example in printing techniques.

While in general, mentors' involvement with students as they actually carried out their tasks was minimal, a few activities were devised where the mentor or class teacher worked alongside the student supporting her and 'guiding her seeing'. One mentor commented,

> I'd like to work with her … I have ideas in my mind as to what I want her to get out of it … what I want her to reach. I think she would just sit there and sop it up and accept it if I said do this and do that. But I don't want to do it, I want her to reach that conclusion.

Towards the end of the project one activity was felt by all the mentors to be particularly worthwhile. Spread over several weeks, this involved a student in working with groups of children, helping them to plan, write and illustrate their own picture books. It was believed by mentors that this activity was 'relevant and meaningful for both student and pupils, and gradually led the student into more sophisticated understandings'; it was 'rich in more complex learning opportunities'. From discussion, it was established that there were limitations in devising activities where the focus of the learning was too narrowly defined. Mentors maintained that what students learned needed to be applicable to other content and useful in other contexts. One mentor commented,

> None of mine could see any links between what they'd done in printing and the rest of the art curriculum ... So, if you only teach tens and units would this knowledge be useful for anything else? What I feel I did was not interchangeable with anything else, the students learned some very specific skills but it didn't take them any further.

In making judgements about 'worthwhile' and 'effective' activities, mentors were also touching on questions of what aspects of subject knowledge might be focused on within the school context. Should activities, for example, focus on developing students' personal subject knowledge or are there other aspects of subject knowledge that are more appropriate for students to learn during school experience? What are teachers' attitudes towards subject knowledge, both in their own teaching and in pupil learning? The next section attempts to explore these questions.

Thinking about subject knowledge

In order to clarify our thinking, one of the first tasks of the action research group was to try and define the content and nature of teachers' subject knowledge and make judgements about what aspects of this knowledge might be mentored in schools. Having consulted and discussed relevant research findings, mentors maintained that because of the holistic and interrelated nature of teaching, they did not consider it appropriate, nor in the school context the best use of time, for subject mentoring to be focused solely on developing students' personal subject knowledge. Rather, they maintained, it should also focus on three other forms of teachers' knowledge: pedagogical content knowledge, general pedagogical knowledge and practical content knowledge. Pedagogical content knowledge is a term used by Shulman (1986) to describe the ways of representing the subject in order to make it accessible to pupils. This form of knowledge will therefore incorporate an understanding of, for example, the most useful and powerful illustrations and analogies, and of pupils' likely conceptions and preconceptions. General pedagogical knowledge was defined by mentors as that knowledge about teaching and pupil learning which was not subject specific, while the term practical content knowledge was used to describe an understanding of how to organise and manage the teaching of a practical activity associated with a subject area – for example, how to manage a practical scientific investigation.

One of the five mentors focused her activities specifically and solely on pedagogical content knowledge: how handwriting is taught, pupils' common difficulties with handwriting and useful 'remedies'. The other mentors appeared to have more complex aims for their students' learning and drew on several forms of subject-related knowledge. Over time, two of these projects in particular became more closely focused on general pedagogical knowledge, and through this focus, on child-centred approaches to teaching and pupil learning. One mentor commented,

> I wanted to see whether she (the student) feels young children can be involved in a geographical subject ... the language of geography, that area. But I don't want her to do it as a subject ... I wanted her not to dismiss them as young children. It doesn't matter how young they are, this has a value for them.

Eventually this mentor commented that she wanted 'to bring it right round to the fact that you can't "teach" geography, it has to be a "hands on" practical activity for very young children'.

Similarly, the mentor who chose to focus on the importance of talking and discussion in mathematical activities maintained,

> I want them to understand that talking is an essential part of learning and that children need to be able to verbalise their thoughts. It was meant to be talking in maths but I couldn't stick to that ... I felt much more comfortable when I let it slip into oracy in general.

For most mentors the activities they devised reflected their commitment (and in some cases their increasing commitment) to child-centred values in primary teaching. This commitment is particularly interesting when considering the apparent changes in mentors' attitudes towards the importance of subject knowledge.

Attitudes towards subject knowledge

When mentors were initially asked to focus their activities on developing students' understanding of subject knowledge their responses had been tough and uncompromising. The importance of subject knowledge was dismissed for themselves and for their pupils – particularly for younger children. Mentors adopted what might be described as a typical child-centred stance: they maintained that the content should not be constrained by the imposition of subject demands and subject boundaries. One mentor commented, 'I felt bullied into choosing a subject, I didn't want to choose a subject at all because I feel strongly that early years aren't about subjects'. Another maintained, 'I just don't think about things as subjects. I know it sounds silly but I don't think, oh my God I've got to teach this science ... it just doesn't feel very sciencey'.

What pupils learned was ultimately regarded as less important than the *way* in which they learned and how far these approaches contributed to enabling pupils to become enthusiastic and independent learners. Mentors commented, for example, 'Does it matter how you get there if the children are enthused?' and 'I'm not interested in them just being able to do blah, blah, blah. I want them to be independent'. As in a previous project (Furlong and Maynard, 1995) mentors also maintained that the content of their activities and their practice were determined not merely by their intentions in terms of pupils' intellectual learning but also by pupils' other needs, for example, their social, emotional and moral development.

But mentors had other, more personal objections to focusing on subject knowledge: they recognised that there were gaps in their substantive subject knowledge (such as facts and concepts), especially in maths and science. These difficulties were particularly apparent to the Key Stage 2 teachers. They commented, for example,

> I feel it's quite difficult doing maths this year with Year 6. Some of the concepts ... you just have to go and swot up on it, read about it and work it out for yourself. I could never do percentages and I can't do them now. In fact I keep a paper in front of me so I can work it out.

Another said,

> When I was in Year 6 I felt I needed to keep one step ahead of my children in science. I'm not a science expert. If I knew what I was going to do in my topic I would research it first so that I could answer some of their questions, not all of them ... have a basic knowledge.

But it was not only with their substantive knowledge of subject areas that mentors had difficulties. Mentors also found they were unable to bring to their consciousness and articulate how the activities they devised for their students reflected more principled theoretical subject understandings. These understandings incorporated knowledge of the subject's key ideas and concepts, its underlying processes, beliefs about the nature of the subject area, and also about why the subject area is considered to be important in pupils' development. One mentor commented,

> What's struck me the more I've talked to people about this is how hidden inside teachers are the reasons why we teach anything. I wasn't alone in not really being able to say clearly what I did printing for. Is the information there but it's so underneath that we just don't recognise it, or don't people know?

This mentor eventually maintained that when she reviewed the activities she planned for her pupils these understandings were 'all there', they had merely been assimilated as generalised approaches to teaching and were therefore unavailable to conscious thought. Others, however, maintained that they had never held these understandings. One mentor commented,

> I don't know why I do half the things I do. I do them because it seems like a good idea at the time ... If someone asks me why do you do it, I just wouldn't

be able to give them an answer. My answer would be, it says I've got to do it in the National Curriculum or I've done it before and it worked really well and the children got a lot out of it. But I wouldn't know intellectual reasons why I did certain things. And I don't think most teachers do.

All the mentors maintained that it was, in any case, simply unfair to expect them to have a thorough and conceptual understanding of all ten National Curriculum areas (including Welsh) and of Religious Education. One mentor commented,

I think in the end what I am going *against* rather than going *for* is that we can't be subject specialists in all eleven subjects. It's impossible. So instead of trying to say 'Yes we must strive towards this' we have to say 'We don't need to strive towards this'.

Indeed, it was the National Curriculum that was often blamed for poor practice, not only in that it forced teachers to cover content superficially but in that it required them to teach topics about which they had little understanding. As one mentor commented,

I did science before the National Curriculum but I only taught science that I understood. But now I have to teach certain aspects of science that I don't understand and I can't do it. I had a terrible lesson the other day in the differences between solids and liquids and gases. And I could define solids and liquids, no problem, but when it came to gases, I just went to pieces. And I could see the look in the children's faces as I lost them totally. And I thought, I'm not surprised that I lost you because I've lost me as well.

Mentors' objections to subject knowledge also appeared to be influenced by their simplistic understandings about this knowledge. For example, mentors tended to equate all subject knowledge with factual knowledge and ways of teaching that were 'more about pushing facts in'. A comment was made that, 'It would be more like a factory … you put this bit in here and that bit in there and what comes out …'. Focusing on subject knowledge was therefore seen to threaten one of the basic tenets of the child-centred approach: the desire to create meaning.

Changing attitudes

During the group meetings, mentors frequently discussed their understandings of subject knowledge. In addition their attitudes towards the importance of subject knowledge in their teaching and in pupils' development were constantly challenged. These challenges were seen as of particular importance by one Key Stage 1 teacher. She maintained that the reason she had never considered the significance of subject knowledge in her teaching was that in working with very young children, the subject knowledge she needed in order to teach effectively was essentially 'common-sense'. This mentor stated,

It is only through the project and looking closely at the students who have got holes in their subject knowledge, that I can see it now. At Key Stage 1 I didn't come up against the content, so I didn't see teaching as needing any knowledge about subjects.

Over time, mentors gradually began to see subject knowledge in more complex ways. For example, they began to discuss the nature of knowledge both in different subject areas and within each subject area. Mentors also began to review their attitudes towards the importance of subject knowledge in primary school teaching. Interestingly, it was the broader, more 'theoretical' subject principles (that they had found so hard to articulate in respect of their own activities) that mentors eventually maintained were of fundamental importance for student teachers to understand. One mentor maintained,

Students need to learn … what is important is the value of the subject … that's the baseline. They need to have a sense of what the subject is and why it is important.

Moreover, attitudes and processes they had been eager to promote – enthusiasm, independence, thinking – but which had been 'free-floating', now became rooted in subject knowledge. For example, teachers who were enthusiastic and inspired enthusiasm in their pupils were seen as 'someone who knew their subject inside out'. Similarly, instead of wanting the children to become 'thinkers' mentors now maintained that they wanted pupils 'to think like mathematicians' and 'to think like scientists'.

Mentors also began to interpret students' 'difficulties' in new ways. They maintained that previously they had not even considered lack of subject knowledge when students had problems with their practice. For example,

I don't know what I used to think students were lacking … perhaps knowledge about pupil learning. I wasn't in touch with the subject.

Lack of subject knowledge, it was claimed, now 'made sense of a lot of things that students do wrong'.

But it was not only students' practice that mentors began to see in new ways. One mentor commented in terms of her own understandings,

I had seen it as general knowledge about teaching. Now I see it as knowledge about the subject which enables me to plan effective teaching from it.

At the end of the project, mentors did not appear to have changed their fundamental attitudes towards what was important about primary teaching. Rather, they had found ways in which to integrate their more complex understandings about subject knowledge into their child-centred thinking and practice. Pupils' intellectual learning did not take precedence over their social and moral development but was eventually seen as being of equal importance. As one mentor maintained, 'It's got to be a balance at primary level, between the content … and … the values and attitudes and ways of working are equally important'. Another commented,

> If the children came out without knowledge in certain subject areas then, even if they came out keen and enthusiastic, I would still think I hadn't done my job, I had failed somewhere. But equally if they had just been prepared for Key Stage 2 with no understanding, no way of using that information, equally I would feel I'd failed.

So much for mentors' thinking and changing attitudes towards subject knowledge. What were the difficulties of implementing subject mentoring in the primary school? What new knowledge and skills did subject mentors need to learn? The next section – difficulties and demands – will explore two areas seen as of particular significance: working with colleagues and working with students.

Difficulties and demands

Working with colleagues

As students undertook their two main block practices in the same school it was inevitable that, at some stage, they would be based in other teachers' classrooms. When this was the case, it was generally decided that students should carry out their tasks in those classrooms. This meant that colleagues needed to become involved: either in allowing mentors to come into their classrooms to work with students or in actually taking a more active role in subject mentoring.

The anticipation of involving colleagues appeared to cause mentors some anxiety. Some of these anxieties were personal and focused on concerns about particular colleagues' reactions. Generally though, anxieties were more concerned with 'professional' issues. For example, mentors recognised that their colleagues were already under a great deal of pressure and were hesitant to ask them to take on more work. Anxieties were also felt when it was believed that other staff had ways of working or priorities that were different from their own, although mentors were eager not to be seen to make judgements on what colleagues did or did not do. In one mentor's words they were 'concerned about appearing to question colleagues' professionalism' .

In reality, with sensitive handling, anticipated difficulties proved to be minimal. However, mentors *did* experience difficulties with a small number of their colleagues and occasionally these difficulties bordered on outright animosity. Sometimes this animosity was felt to be directed at them personally – for example, mentors' involvement with the project was described by colleagues as 'time off'. On other occasions colleagues expressed their resentment about what was seen as the mentor's interference with 'their' student. Hostility was also directed towards the principle of being involved in subject mentoring. One mentor maintained,

> When we were developing a programme for students I felt there was a lot of support, people felt it was a really good idea, whereas ... I think they're basically so against mentoring subject knowledge ... they feel it is quite, quite wrong that schools should get involved in this. My colleagues feel that if we make it work then next term they'll say, no time out of school to do this but here you are.

In general, however, mentors faced neither enthusiasm nor animosity but simple lack of interest. For example, one mentor maintained,

> Actually I did try to involve the maths co-ordinator but I scored a definite deaf ear there. I didn't come out saying 'Will you help me with this?' but I started to explain what I was doing and got a definite ... 'no interest'.

Another mentor commented,

> There are certain things that I have to discuss and certain things that I want to find out and I need to talk to the class teacher. And I'm not saying they don't view it seriously .... But it's very much – 'You're doing that. Get on with it, it's your pigeon'.

Mentors maintained that if they were to gain support from colleagues for this work – and this was believed to be of fundamental importance if subject mentoring was to be effective – then student teachers had to become a priority within the school. The importance of the headteacher's attitude in this respect was often stressed, although mentors emphasised that headteachers would not see students as a priority when the school was involved in major change or had other pressing priorities such as inspection. One mentor commented about her own school,

> There were always other things that took priority at staff meetings. We're in a state of flux in the school, we're making major changes and this basically has come at the wrong time.

Whole school support for subject mentoring was believed to be of particular importance in small schools where colleagues' lack of interest was more visible and placed greater demands on the remaining members of staff. As one mentor explained,

> With a bigger school you can afford to carry one or two teachers who aren't interested, but in a small school if one of your teachers doesn't want to do it that's a third of your school.

In the end, involving colleagues in this work was not an area in which most mentors felt they had been particularly successful. Mentors had set tasks which students carried out without support in their own classrooms and which were then discussed by mentor and student in the feedback session. In general therefore, colleagues' involvement with subject mentoring was minimal.

Working with students

As mentors began to clarify and refine the purposes of their activities, they also became aware that mentoring subject knowledge required them to do more than merely support students' practical learning: it required them to take on the role of 'teacher'. This realisation was gradual and in the early stages of their work with students, mentors did not make use of the pedagogical knowledge they had developed in working with pupils. Unsurprisingly then, their difficulties and learning processes were similar to those experienced by student teachers at the beginning of their school experience. For example, while initially mentors had been concerned with 'how they were going to convey all this information', later on they began to realise 'the importance of a clear, tight focus'.

Mentors also recognised that if they were to take on the role of 'teacher' then they needed to develop similar kinds of understandings about student teachers as those which they held about pupils. When planning activities, for example, mentors maintained they relied heavily on their knowledge of the particular pupils in their class and of pupils' 'likely' responses and difficulties. Moreover, they held understandings about how pupils best learn and how to support, guide, structure and direct this learning. This *kind* of knowledge, mentors maintained, was also fundamental to – but lacking in – their work with student teachers. One mentor commented,

> I don't think I know the students as well as the children in my class, I don't know how they set about things, I just haven't had enough time with them. I don't know them as people, I don't know them as learners.

A key issue in this respect was gaining an understanding of their students' perspectives – what the students themselves felt they wanted. These 'wants', as mentors described them, centred primarily on the development of students' own practical knowledge – how to teach and how to survive the next day. Students made it clear that they were unhappy about being involved in any activities that diverted their focus away from this learning or took them out of *their* classrooms. One mentor explained,

> To take them away from their class and their class teacher is, they feel, taking them away from where their learning is. It's their 'wants', they want to be left in the classroom to learn from their own mistakes.

Another mentor maintained her students had stated, 'Just leave us alone, let us stay in the classroom, you keep stopping us learning.'

But if they were to plan appropriate and effective activities, then as well as considering students' 'wants', mentors also felt they had to consider students' broader, longer term learning 'needs'. These needs were considered to be primarily concerned with the development of more complex understandings about how pupils learn. However, as mentors' attitudes towards the importance of subject knowledge changed, student teachers' 'needs' also incorporated an understanding of the more 'theoretical' and principled understandings about subject areas.

Trying to find ways in which to draw in these more 'theoretical' understandings when students were so focused on their own personal, practical learning posed a real problem. In general, mentors attempted to resolve this difficulty by overtly focusing their activities on meeting students' 'wants' – *how* to teach – while at opportune moments (usually in feedback sessions) attempting to discuss *why* the activity could be considered appropriate and effective. As one mentor explained,

> I think you've got to use their interest in how to do it … divert … slip in there some of the things that you want under the guise of what *they* want.

Another mentor commented,

> For them it's very practical. What they see it as, is giving them skills and knowledge about different methods of teaching printmaking …. and then I'm going to pull out, help them to see *why* it was important.

The term 'stealthy mentor' was coined to epitomise the way in which mentors felt they had to work.

However, becoming a 'teacher' was not only an issue in terms of the content of activities but also in terms of the role mentors felt they had to adopt when working with students. As stated earlier, mentors were being asked to work not only as subject mentors but also as class mentors and senior mentors. As class mentors it was felt that there was a need to maintain a close supportive relationship with students. In being a senior mentor, and in particular, in mentoring subject knowledge, they came to realise that there was a need to establish a quite different relationship.

All the mentors complained about student teachers' reluctance to complete the tasks that were set for them. For example, one mentor commented,

> For weeks and weeks they wouldn't do it. We set deadlines and they would always have an excuse why they hadn't done it.

Moreover, in the debriefing sessions where mentors intended to explore the broader principles underlying students' tasks it was felt that, however carefully these were structured, students refused to focus on anything but their own agenda: the development of practical knowledge. One mentor maintained,

> I'm concerned I'm not doing enough. She's saying 'Yes, yes' then 'What do we do about this?' She goes back to what *she* wants, not what *I* want each time.

Mentors gradually became aware that if they were to be effective as subject mentors they needed to be much more formal, structured and interventionist. They also realised that if they were to be 'teachers' of students then they needed to gain control: to establish their authority and retain a professional distance. However, mentors maintained they faced certain difficulties in this respect.

Firstly, as part of a research project this work was seen by students as an 'extra'. Mentors commented that they felt acutely aware of any additional demands they were making of student teachers. One mentor commented,

> I felt guilty about asking them to do this and I found myself almost thanking them for doing this for me.

When students were based in mentors' classes, the conflicting demands of the roles of class mentor and subject mentor caused tensions and also militated against them taking a more authoritative stance. As one mentor commented,

> It's hard to be a class mentor *and* a subject mentor because as class mentor you're very involved with the student. You're blowing hot and cold. One minute you're this very supportive, kindly teacher and the next minute you've got to put this other hat on. And I think that could cause problems. I don't think the subject mentor can also be a class mentor.

The number of students in the school was also seen as significant in terms of mentors' ease with establishing their authority. Where there was only one student in the school, even when they were working in another class, there was the tendency for the mentor–student relationship 'to be more personal'. Unsurprisingly therefore, mentors maintained that there were many advantages to working with a group of students.

Finally, mentors believed that they had difficulties in this respect simply because neither they, nor the students, perceived class teachers – even class teachers acting as mentors – as having the right to establish authority over student teachers. As one mentor explained,

> The students don't visualise us as having authority ... it's not only our perception it's theirs as well. They don't think we have authority. When we ask them to do an exercise by a certain date they think, well as long as I get the university stuff done.

Mentors maintained that if they were to be effective in mentoring subject knowledge then the schools needed to have, and be seen to have, the same authority over student teachers as the university. As one mentor maintained,

> Students have got to know that this isn't something that we're asking you to do to fill in a bit of your time, this is important and you've got to do it. And it's not a matter of 'We'd like you to do it by next week if you can find the time', 'You *will* do it by next Tuesday and if you don't then you're going to fail'.

However, while they were willing to explore the issue of authority in 'theory', in 'practice' several of the mentors expressed a personal reluctance to take on a more authoritative role. As one commented,

> I don't like being authoritarian – it's because they're another adult. That's the conflict. They're intelligent people and I wouldn't feel comfortable with that.

Another mentor maintained,

> I think it's got to do with you as a person. You want the students to like you – you don't want to go in with a big stick. To get the best out of anybody you have to be approachable and let them know you're on their side. And I think there's a bit of conflict there from being supportive and friendly in that way to having to go in and criticise their practice. That's not a role I feel happy with at the moment.

Having explored some of the difficulties and demands of mentoring subject knowledge, I now return to examine mentors' attitudes towards subject mentoring at the conclusion of the project.

Teachers' attitudes towards subject mentoring

Towards the end of the project, mentors' commitment to subject mentoring hit a low point; they began to have severe doubts about the appropriateness and relevance of mentoring subject knowledge in the primary school. Partly this seemed to stem from their feelings of exhaustion and stress – they found it difficult to cope with all the demands (and conflicting demands) that being a class mentor, senior mentor and subject mentor made of them. As practising teachers, even being released from teaching for a half day a week was not enough to meet the requirements of mentoring. Time was needed, they constantly pointed out, not only for working with student teachers but also for liaising with the university tutor, for reading and researching, for preparation, for giving feedback, and, importantly, for working with colleagues.

However, giving teachers more 'bought-out' time was not seen as the solution. Mentors maintained that teachers did not want time away from their classes: the relationship they built up with their pupils was of fundamental importance to them, both personally and professionally. One mentor commented,

> Being out of the class for half a day a week seems to me to make no difference but if you were out of the class for more than that then they cease to be your class in the same way as they are when you are there all the time.

The demands of subject mentoring were believed to be of particular significance to mentors working in small schools. It was not that there was a lack of subject expertise within small schools, but that they suffered from 'overload'. They suffered from 'curriculum overload' – they were responsible for up to four curriculum areas and had to write and oversee the implementation of school policies for each of these. Further, both individual teachers and schools suffered from 'student overload' and this was seen as having important implications both for teachers' own 'job satisfaction' and for pupil learning. Moreover, as there were fewer opportunities for non-contact time in small schools, this time was used for what were seen as high priority issues. As one mentor commented, 'Mentoring, which you could say was optional, doesn't have a show.'

But mentoring subject knowledge was also, as noted earlier, demanding of teachers in other ways, including their understanding of the principles underlying their activities. Their initial inability to locate these understandings had left many mentors feeling vulnerable and inadequate. For example, one mentor maintained,

> My idea was that subjects were basically irrelevant to early years children. What was important was ways of working, attitudes and skills. Students had to think about how children learned. Everything had to be planned that way. I never though any further than that, Well suddenly I realise that there's that other element to it. It's really shaken me. If I had not seen the relevance of subject knowledge what else didn't I know? I really felt clear about what I knew – and there was this big thing I'd never thought about ... Why didn't I know about this? Why had I left this big gap there?

Ultimately, when they reviewed the forms of subject-related knowledge, it was not personal subject knowledge but those aspects that were essentially centred on their general, practical knowledge (pedagogical content knowledge, practical content knowledge and general pedagogical knowledge) that mentors claimed they felt most comfortable mentoring. As one mentor explained,

> *How* you teach tens and units, *how* you set up the classroom to teach tens and units ... and the general knowledge about teaching and learning, that comes into it too.

Teachers did not have the time or the expertise, it was felt, to focus on the principles underlying activities – particularly those related to subject knowledge. Mentors commented,

> I can't see the point of people who are not subject specialists doing 'What is the nature of the subject?' It's not what we're good at.

Another mentor maintained that her colleagues had stated,

> We don't know anything about subjects, we're not subject specialists. I wouldn't mind telling them how to develop creative writing but I wouldn't like to talk about why creative writing is important.

But it was not only mentors who had difficulty in this respect. Despite students' assurances that they 'already knew what the subject area was about', mentors maintained that in fact, students' knowledge of these more 'theoretical' subject understandings appeared limited or even non-existent. For example, when in the feedback session one mentor had tried to 'connect' the practical task students had undertaken in print making with what she believed were key ideas about art and art education, students had appeared to have no knowledge of these ideas. This mentor commented,

> I took it at face value that they knew all about art because they said they did. And they didn't.

While mentors maintained that it was fundamentally important for students to consider these more principled understandings when planning activities for pupils, at the same time they questioned the appropriateness of subject mentoring for student teachers at this point in their professional development. One mentor maintained,

> I don't think students are really interested … I know it's important but I think it's something you could do with them as newly qualified teachers rather than now. We're trying to spend so much time mentoring one tiny specific aspect, and you think there's so much more they need to know. I don't feel I can keep pushing that little bit because they're not interested really. They say, 'We agree, it's important, we'll do it' but they're not interested and I feel I'm flogging a dead horse basically.

Unsurprisingly then, despite the apparent shifts in their attitudes towards subject knowledge, it was believed that subject mentoring took up time that mentors would much rather spend on more general and child-centred aspects of their practice. As one mentor commented,

> I know why we've done subject mentoring but in some ways I feel frustrated like they do … what I would really like to spend time doing is not this subject bit. It's been like an irritation. I'm conscious of so many other things that they needed that I could have done something about.

Mentoring subject knowledge had demanded a great deal and had apparently achieved very little. Subject mentoring, it was maintained, would only be worthwhile if activities were more 'cost effective' – less demanding of mentors and of more profound influence and importance in students' learning. As one mentor commented,

> We've spent an enormous amount of time on something quite small. And if it's going to work then you're going to have to do something which is less time consuming or more useful for the students in other contexts … And what about everything else they ought to be learning?

Conclusion

The way in which mentors devised and implemented their activities and the roles that they developed in working with students were, to an extent, idiosyncratic – built around and constrained by their individual personalities and understandings as teachers, and the particular contexts in which they were working. Moreover, some of the difficulties mentors faced were, it appeared, specifically related to, or were exacerbated by, the fact that as part of a research project their work lacked official status. However, when returning to our initial three questions, certain broad conclusions and implications can be drawn from this project.

What aspects of subject knowledge might be mentored in the primary school?

In attempting to define those aspects of subject knowledge that might be mentored in the primary school, several factors appear to be of significance. These factors are diverse. They relate to the nature of teachers' knowledge, teachers' values, student teachers' demands and needs, teachers' subject knowledge, and also to the nature of subject knowledge itself.

Firstly, teaching is complex and as our mentors emphasised, aspects of teachers' knowledge are interrelated. It may therefore be inappropriate to extract one aspect of teachers' knowledge and aim to develop this in isolation from the rest of students' practice. Moreover, focusing solely on students' personal subject knowledge would not appear to be the best use of the school context. It does seem appropriate, therefore, that in terms of subject mentoring 'subject knowledge' should be more broadly defined as 'subject-related' knowledge, that is, knowledge related to the teaching of subjects. However, it is noted that adopting this broader definition of 'subject knowledge' did allow mentors to focus their activities on general pedagogical knowledge, or more specifically on developing students' understandings of child-centred approaches to teaching and pupil learning.

Students' perspectives – their 'wants' – may also need to be considered. Students, it was discovered, were reluctant to focus on anything but the development of their own practical knowledge. Students claimed that while they understood something of the nature, key ideas and purposes of subject areas this was of little relevance when faced with a class of 30 children – what they needed to know was how to teach and how to survive.

A further consideration relates to teachers' subject knowledge. Mentors acknowledged their own lack of substantive knowledge of concepts and procedures in certain curriculum areas particularly at Key Stage 2. Mentors also had difficulty in locating the broader, more 'theoretical' subject principles underlying the activities they taught. Ultimately, these particular understandings were considered by mentors to be of fundamental importance to student teachers. Mentors maintained that without this knowledge, students' activities could easily become superficial and trivial. Mentors' attempts to help students evaluate their practical tasks in terms of these particular understandings had not, in general, been successful – in part because of lack of time and student interest but also because students appeared to lack this knowledge. While this may have been the case, it could equally have been a reflection of students' difficulties in relating 'theoretical' college-based learning to 'action' (Russell, 1988; Calderhead, 1988), or simply recalling theoretical understandings in the classroom context.

One further factor needs to be taken into consideration. Mentors maintained that there may be a danger in making the focus of student learning too narrow and specific. In part, this is a question of logistics – too prescribed or tight a focus in terms of substantive content may indicate the necessity for subject mentoring to be carried out within a particular class. The effectiveness of subject mentoring would thus become reliant on one teacher's particular perspective, understandings and goodwill in undertaking this work. Further, focusing on a narrowly-defined concept or procedure may not provide students with the opportunity to gain understandings which are applicable to other concepts and other contexts.

Defining those aspects of subject knowledge that might be mentored in schools is thus a complex task. One possible solution might be for teachers to mentor those aspects of subject-related knowledge about which they feel they have the most expertise and which student teachers maintained were of most immediate relevance to them: pedagogical content knowledge, general pedagogical knowledge and practical content knowledge. Activities might focus not on specific, narrowly-defined concepts or procedures but on key ideas, associated skills and underlying processes associated with the subject area. For example, an activity might aim to develop students' understanding of how to teach, manage and organise a scientific investigation. Teachers would then be free to incorporate that content which is considered particularly challenging and informative for student teachers given the mentor's expertise and the particular context in which the student is working.

What are the possibilities, demands and constraints of mentoring subject knowledge in the primary school?

Teachers' understandings about pupil learning, and their growing knowledge about mentoring strategies are, mentors came to realise, useful and 'relevant' to mentoring subject knowledge. Considering the strength of teachers' child-centred beliefs, it is unsurprising that what mentors ultimately considered to be a 'good' activity rested on the same underlying principles that they applied to their work with pupils: the activity was presented as an 'experience', it had a real purpose and the learning was contextualised, carefully supported and structured. The effectiveness of the activity in developing student teachers' subject understandings did not appear, for the majority of mentors, to be a priority: they did not appear to have become 'subject-centred'.

Where mentors were willing to take on a more formal interventionist stance, had a supportive headteacher and were able to gain the interest of colleagues, it appeared that mentoring subject knowledge afforded considerable potential for professional development. Indeed, one of the mentors was able to persuade two colleagues to run workshop sessions for students on their particular areas of expertise. These sessions, which focused on good practice in special needs teaching and art were also attended by several teaching colleagues.

While the possibilities of mentoring subject knowledge were acknowledged by mentors, the tensions, difficulties and demands of this work were also recognised. As we have seen, one of the most commonly mentioned demands and constraints was time. In addition, mentors discovered there were many organisational demands. For example, as subject mentoring was found to be more effective when mentors worked with groups of students and when the subject mentor was not also the student's class mentor, questions were raised about the feasibility of subject mentoring in smaller schools where staff already appear to suffer from curriculum and student overload.

However, some of the most profound difficulties and tensions appeared to centre on teachers' attitudes and beliefs. It was noted that most mentors essentially focused their activities on helping students to develop 'general pedagogical knowledge' – specifically an understanding of child-centred ways of teaching. It was noted that, as the project progressed, two mentors increasingly saw this aspect as of importance despite their claims that they now acknowledged the importance of subject knowledge for themselves, student teachers and pupils. At the end of the project it was unclear whether mentors' continued emphasis on developing students' child-centred understandings represented their real attitudes towards subject knowledge; their difficulties in assimilating their changed attitudes into their day to day practice; their priorities for student teachers' learning while on their school experience; or, indeed some other factor. What could be ascertained, however, was the difficulty in changing primary teachers' practice.

Teachers' attitudes towards the 'ownership' of classrooms, pupils and student teachers also appeared to be a fundamental constraint on mentoring subject knowledge in the primary school. Mentors recognised that teachers often saw their classrooms as 'their own little world' and that this perspective was also extended to the way they viewed their students. They were also concerned that working with students in colleagues' classrooms might be seen as 'questioning colleagues' professionalism'. Moreover, despite the time needed to mentor subject knowledge effectively, mentors maintained that teachers would not be willing to spend more than half a day away from 'their' classes. For subject mentoring to be effective, it was recognised that there needed to be a general willingness to 'open doors' – both in discussing practice and in relinquishing ownership of student teachers and pupils. It is again difficult to see how these attitudes, which appear to be so bound up in the whole culture of primary schools, could easily change. An important conclusion of this project therefore, is that teachers' attitudes, supported as they are by the culture of the primary school, may be one of the major constraints on mentoring subject knowledge in the primary school.

If it is the belief of the government that the introduction of subject mentoring will simply 'encourage' teachers to adopt a more subject-centred approach to their teaching, then there may have been a misunderstanding of the strength of primary teachers' commitment to the child-centred ideology. Any attempt to change teachers' practice – that is to change their values – by imposition, or even by persuasion of individual teachers, may well founder.

What are the implications of subject mentoring for schools and higher education institutions?

Mentors ultimately maintained that there is a need for student teachers, while on their school experience, to focus on more than just 'how to teach' subject-related knowledge. Student teachers, it was recognised, also need to be challenged to evaluate the way in which the activities they devise for their pupils relate to or reflect broader, more principled understandings about the subject area in which they are working. Mentors' difficulties with subject knowledge – that is, their attitudes towards subject knowledge, their understanding of substantive content, and their understanding of the more theoretical subject principles underlying their activities – and their reticence to take on a more authoritative role in their work with student teachers appear to indicate the need for the continued involvement of the HEI tutor in students' school-based work (Maynard, 1995).

If schools do take on a more structured and systematic approach to developing students' practical understandings of subject-related knowledge, this may also have implications for the content of college-based studies. It has been recognised that the focus of college-based studies has, in recent years, increasingly become concerned with what are seen as 'practical' issues (Furlong et al., 1994). It could be argued that students' tentative hold on the subject principles underlying their activities was, in one sense, a reflection and consequence of this concern. If the distinctive roles and contributions of schools and higher education institutions were more clearly defined, then there may be a need to review this focus.

It would, however, be unwise to prescribe the exact parameters of the contribution of schools and higher education institutions to subject mentoring. Mentors maintained that if subject mentoring *is* to be imposed on them by the government, while the activities they mentor may aim to contextualise and enhance college-based studies, any programme has to be developed in equal partnership between schools and HEIs. One mentor commented,

> I don't want the college to say 'You will do'... it's got to be mutually agreed. I'd like to be able to say 'Well I feel I could do ... I am in a better position to explore this area and you are in a better position to explore the other'. I think there has to be a greater liaison so school and college don't see each other as a threat.

Postscript: February 1995

Six months after the project had ended, mentors were busy working with new groups of students in their schools. It appeared that, for two of the mentors in particular, there was a real willingness to implement and develop understandings gained from the project. One mentor commented that she was trying to establish a more authoritative role with the students in her school. Another, who had in the previous year managed to gain the interest and support of some her colleagues, spoke with enthusiasm of 'real changes within the school'. Colleagues, she maintained, were becoming much more interventionist in their work with student teachers and were beginning to open doors and discuss their practice. She added however, 'We're not mentoring subject knowledge though, just our general practice'.

During their involvement in the project, mentors had commented that in the face of constant change and overwhelming demands, if nothing else, primary teachers had learnt how to manipulate in order to survive. As one mentor had wryly commented, 'Primary teachers always find ways of doing more of the things they like and less of the things they don't like.' This, it appears, may also may be the case with mentoring subject knowledge in the primary school.

CHAPTER 4

Subject Perspectives in Mentoring

Lisa Dart and Pat Drake

Introduction

'I love my subject' is often the answer applicants for English PGCE places give to: 'Why do you want to teach English?' Mathematicians respond in more cerebral ways such as: 'I like problem-solving', or state with confidence 'I'm good at maths'. We have yet to hear anyone in an English interview make any comments about capability in their subject. Usually they are much more concerned to convince of their suitability by emphasising their passion for literature and their commitment to continuing to read ever more widely. Interestingly, and perhaps not surprisingly, English mentors, when interviewed about qualities they sought in teachers of their subject, stressed exactly the same thing, favouring, as they expressed it, people who love literature. It is clear that this feeling about their subject is seen as an essential requirement for teaching. It does not seem to be the case for mathematics teachers: they sought teachers who were flexible and willing to learn on the hoof (Drake and Dart 1994).

How then do these very different attributes come to be assessed using the competence model outlined by the Department for Education in Circular No 9/92 (1992)? Can the same statements of competence be applied systematically across all of the curriculum subjects regardless of these and other complicating factors, such as different types of pupils and mentors, or varied contexts and levels of resourcing? What are the assumptions and beliefs that teachers have about their subject which inform their judgements regarding student teacher competence? Are these assumptions and beliefs about what it is to be a good teacher of their subject made clear to the students? And, importantly, do they influence the process of assessment of student teachers positively or not? It would seem that, from the responses they made at initial interview, intending teachers already have an implicit sense of what is expected for teaching their particular subject and they often seek for it to be confirmed in the schools in which they train.

Mentors and tutors in both schools and HEIs may, of course, share students' implicit sense of their subject; but again they might not. Does it matter and how do we know whether they do or not ? As one might expect, understanding the effects of underlying subject assumptions on the process of training generally, and assessment particularly, is central to the changing relationship between schools and HEIs. In this chapter, we look at both student teachers' subject experience prior to PGCE and subject cultures in school, and consider possible mismatch between student and mentor subject perception. We draw upon tape recorded mentor sessions[1] between seven mentor–student pairs, three in English and four in mathematics. Prior to this, all mentors had been interviewed as part of the project and had subsequently agreed to record their sessions with their students. From this research we argue that without examination of implicit subject philosophies, many opportunities for intellectual and professional development are missed; and that, where a student and a mentor appear to have different beliefs, it may well threaten their professional relationship, often to the detriment of the student.

Student teachers' experience

Inevitably, the responses at interview of those applying for PGCE courses are, probably to a large extent, the result of what they have absorbed from their own experience at school and university. They have already gained some sense of their subject's culture. So, at the outset of their PGCE course, they already have their own sets of beliefs and values about teaching their subject, as well, of course, powerful images of what it is to be an effective teacher (Calderhead, 1991). One mentor commented,

> Someone comes in and they think a good teacher is the best teacher I had. So what they are trying to do is turn into something they have a stereo-typical image of … (mathematics mentor, male, Head of Department)

It is unrealistic to assume that dovetailing will, or indeed should, always occur between a student's and, a mentor's subject beliefs. Eraut (1994) makes the significant point that it is rare for student teachers to be encouraged to scrutinise many of their implicitly held ideas before commencing their teaching. The same, we suggest, is also true for those undertaking mentoring. Not only is it very likely that students of different subjects will have a range of views about what it means to be a teacher; even those in the same discipline will often find themselves in disagreement about what it means to be a good teacher of that subject.

Mentors, then, need to be aware that students' understanding of their subject originates from their own school days and will be, often inextricably, linked to the way it was taught. Since the methods they have experienced can often be adopted as 'the right ones', it is a skilled mentor who will enable the student to approach an area with a different and better pedagogy. Booth *et al.* (1990:103) point out in a study of history PGCE students that even for those wanting to adopt new approaches, it was essential for them to be given the appropriate pedagogical skills.

> What emerged from London and Manchester and from the national survey was that for the overwhelming majority of students their own school history had been didactic, limited in its learning demands and overwhelmingly geared towards examination success. When on teaching practice in schools however they wanted to adopt very different strategies. They were concerned with introducing source materials such as primary written documents, pictures and artefacts. It was vital therefore that they were taught about suitable teaching strategies.

Without the appropriate support it is easy to see how students will fall back on their own experience as learners of their subject and not implement any subject innovations.

So, assuming that all student teachers arrive with their own philosophies about the teaching of their subject, and perhaps, despite Booth *et al.*, the personal attributes necessary for it, if one of the qualities required of English student teachers happens to be a love of literature, how do they show it in school? And how does a mentor recognise it? If a mentor is not convinced of the student's genuine passion for literature how much will it, or indeed should it, influence the judgement about professional competence? Is it easier for some students, whatever their own view of literature, simply to recognise this facet of the subject's culture and merely espouse it?

School and subject culture

In his research into the socialization of doctoral students Gerholm (1985: 26) emphasises the importance of the notion of 'tacit knowledge'. In the case of entry into an academic department, he observes,

> Any person entering a new group with the ambition of becoming a full-fledged, competent member has to learn to comply with its fundamental cultural rules ... To function smoothly, within the group of teachers, fellow students and secretaries, the student needs a considerable amount of know-how. Most of it will be acquired slowly through the interaction with others and without anyone ever making a deliberate effort to teach the newcomer the rules of the game. Nonetheless, failure to comply with these implicit rules will undoubtedly affect the student's standing within the group.

The importance of understanding the culture of the school that you are entering was recognised by mentors as significant in teacher education. One mentor remarked that

I think one of the real issues has to be: how do you give people that are coming into schools access – real access into the culture of the school … It does concern me that at times people come into schools thinking 'I'm going to experience what it is like to be a teacher' and they actually have no access to that experience at all because they aren't equipped for that access. (mathematics mentor, male, Head of Department)

Perhaps those students used to working in other environments quickly see how to work within the cultural behaviour that characterises any professional group. Jargon and its accompanying practices may be, for some, quickly assimilated and just as quickly adopted. For others it may be more difficult simply because they lack experience. Whichever is the case, it seems that success or failure at recognising the kinds of practices to which Gerholm refers – that is gaining understanding of tacit knowledge – will inform decisions about competence. At the outset of their PGCE course students are being introduced to the culture, language and system of education generally. As one mentor suggested:

The real problem is … we live in in our own little environment, our own language, our own signals, our own codes, so that we … I can imagine that someone could walk into the staffroom and think we're actually on another planet because we're talking about [*for example*] an NQT or I was doing an MA … to us it makes sense but to anybody else forget it … it's complete jargon. It's very hard for someone to get into that without the background to it. (mathematics mentor, male, Head of Department)

Although the mentors quoted above were talking about the culture of the school more generally, the same point also applies to the subject culture of departments within schools. When they begin their training, students are also entering into a particular department, one with its own practices for teaching English or mathematics.

Now when we have our faculty meetings talking to other mathematicians we tend to click into our maths jargon. It's very exclusive, very hard for people who aren't used to that … very few people actually understand what we're talking about and that's probably not just true of maths, I think, but of education in general. (mathematics mentor, male, Head of Department)

As Becher (1989:24) comments, 'The professional language and literature of any disciplinary group play a key role in establishing its cultural identity.' Jargon has its own badge of exclusivity but, even without it, distinctive disciplinary groups create their own register which emerges from shared ' traditions, customs, practices, transmitted knowledge, beliefs, morals, and rules of conduct, as well as their linguistic and symbolic forms of communication and meaning'. Mentors recognised that the difficulties students might face in learning about their subject culture were exacerbated by the rapid changes in education.

Well I mean there's been such rapid development recently that it's difficult ...

very hard to keep up with all the changes as well … and it's more difficult for the students. You see they come in … [and] there's a sense in which they're overwhelmed by the demands of the National Curriculum. (English mentor, female, Head of Department)

An ever-increasing amount of jargon was having to be assimilated by both students and mentors alike.

Less experienced students, aware of the audiences that they have had to negotiate at university, may find themselves unsure of how to proceed when it comes to making sense of their subject culture. At university students may have to appear committed to their subject when talking to a tutor, yet the reasons for studying it may be other than love of subject. These can be admitted to peers, admission which might even include 'I hate studying … (whatever text it happens to be)'. Training as a teacher, they will also be expected, in more recent years, to make some sense of the impact of the National Curriculum on their subject. In the HEI this may mean understanding its evolution and political underpinnings; in a school department it will be recognising the departmental view of its worth, and knowing how it is interpreted in preparation and planning. If the role of the mentor is characterised, as it is at the University of Sussex, as that of both assessor and 'critical friend', it may be a difficult one for some students to understand quickly, and they may unintentionally give a wrong impression which may count against them.

Aspects of subject culture

Of course, it need not only be love of literature on which English teachers are judged; other inexplicit criteria may also influence decisions about competence. An English student, for example, is commonly expected to be interested in the theatre and, likely as not, media studies. But what about something less obviously subject-related, such as the kind of flexibility mathematics teachers look for? The last statement of competence under Subject Application requires the 'ability to select and use appropriate resources, including Information Technology' (DfE Circular 9/92 Annex A2.3.7). It is easy to see how students' experience of IT will be dependent on not only the actual level of resources in any one school, but also individual departments' beliefs about its use. As one mentor observed,

It's perfectly possible people come in without big rafts of areas – say on IT – which is you know a major part of the delivery. That's not a problem in the sense that people have got degrees and we assume are capable of learning. The problem is how to facilitate their learning and organise the time for them. (mathematics mentor, male, Head of Department)

Importantly, students may not realise that their responses to these aspects of their subject's culture may well be part of the implicit criteria which inform judgements about competence. Most English departments would probably understand any student's reluctant interest in information technology; the above suggests the opposite would normally be true in mathematics. Suppose that students succeed in mastering these complexities, what then about gaps in their subject knowledge? The statements of competence under subject knowledge are very broad. Newly qualified teachers should be able to demonstrate

> an understanding of the knowledge, concepts and skills of their specialist subjects and of the place of these subjects in the school curriculum: as well as a breadth and depth of subject knowledge extending beyond PoS and examination syllabuses in school. (DfE Circular 9/92, Annex A2.2.1 and A2.2.3 Subject Knowledge)

Within each subject, students' degrees often vary substantially in content. Inevitably some will be better equipped to teach certain curriculum areas than others. This is obvious in history where a student may never have studied a particular period that forms part of a school's curriculum. In both English and mathematics it was apparent that mentors were attuned to the likelihood of subject knowledge gaps in their students. However, this was articulated in ways which pointed up some of the difficulties of separating the two competences. Subject knowledge 'in some contexts appears to denote the particular constellation of ideas, techniques, beliefs and values which serve to define a disciplinary culture' (Becher, 1989:27). Accordingly, while 'gap' was defined as the knowledge a trainee might lack, it was commonly viewed in terms of pedagogical approaches and beliefs as well.

Subject knowledge gap

At one level subject knowledge gap can be seen as the discrepancy between the students' own knowledge and any particular area that is covered on the syllabus with which they are not familiar. Such an area was neither part of their own school experience, their degree, nor any other life experience. Mentors and students both expressed an awareness of this.

> I think there's a problem that they will find lots of school mathematics wasn't what they did at school ... When I was at school ... very traditional lots of sums and things, so that it can be quite a shock ... all these strange problems and things that children do now can be really quite daunting for a student. (mathematics mentor, male, not Head of Department)

> One of the problems with the English degrees is that they tend to be literature-based and so much of the National Curriculum is not literature-based because it includes media, it includes drama and it includes English language ...

Furthermore the kind of literature you study at university tends to be the sort of literature you just might get round to if you're lucky ... in many 11–16 schools they're not studied at all. So I'm aware of that when they come to us. (English mentor, male, Head of Department)

In response to his mentor's questions about quadratic equations, a student said,

I'd considered doing some number patterns which obviously would have quadratic and linear differences running through. Differences are something I've only really come across through my own foster daughter. Despite having a maths degree I never did differences before ... I didn't realise that there are difference equations that follow the same rules as differential equations ... and I thought: why haven't I? I've got a good degree and no one has ever shown me. (mathematics student, male)

In mathematics, students may not be familiar with, for example, a mathematical concept such as standard deviation in statistics. As one mentor said,

When we get to higher levels MA 5 which is our stats ... there will be people teaching things like standard deviation who've never taught it in their lives and may have done it if they were lucky in their degree. The chances are they probably didn't so they're having to almost keep, you know, re-learn. It's not unique to students. You know the curriculum is changing and has changed. (mathematics mentor, male, Head of Department)

However, the imposition of a National Curriculum, with its ensuing changes and redefinitions of subject content, highlights the more complex aspects of defining subject knowledge gap, as well as the equally complex training issues underlying the statements of competence.

Because there's lots of things that have come in and because in the National Curriculum for maths you've got five attainment targets[2] and one of them is statistics and probability – you've got a lot of stuff at the higher end that wasn't on GCSE syllabuses. (mathematics mentor, female, Head of Department)

Quite often changes have also happened during the course of any one academic year. What might be essential subject knowledge one year may be less significant the next, or be omitted altogether. For example, in the case of mathematics there has been considerable controversy over the inclusion of 'Using and Applying Mathematics', and in English heated debate about the changing list of prescribed authors, and the teaching of Standard English. It seems easy, then, to argue simply that students, in mathematics or English, are required to catch up with their verbs, deixis, statistics or whatever. Easy, at least in the sense that an area can be explicitly identified as inadequate and then learnt; not so easy, in that as Booth, et al. (1990:102) comment, a short, intensive PGCE course 'cannot hope to add to the students' knowledge of subject content'. And in fact, catching up could be very difficult for student teachers to manage when there is not only little time, but when the beliefs and assumptions that inform the teaching of such topics are seldom made explicit.

Subject beliefs

To think of subject knowledge gap just as a matter of content is an over-simplification. A subject is not only its content, since in any institution subjects are understood by the practices that surround them. It is the ideas, techniques, beliefs and values, the defining elements of subject knowledge, that may well remain implicit in the training process. Debates about what is taught, how it is taught and why it is taught – the central questions of all teaching – are, for a variety of reasons, often not covered explicitly in mentor–student dialogue. The main factors may simply be time and expectation. In a one-hour mentoring session there is usually a lot to cover, and any wider debate may be seen in the eyes of both mentor and student as more appropriate for the HEI to deal with.

> What's difficult in your mentor time is having enough time if you like to debate philosophy rather than pragmatics -what am I actually going to do with this particular class this week or this day- and a lot of the time we actually spend discussing the lessons, what happened in the lessons and why, rather than if you like the philosophy behind them, simply because of the pressure of time. So thinking back on my mentorship last year that was something that was missing. In a sense I tended to feel well perhaps the university was doing that. The difficulty of being a mentor in school is that you are split. You're aware you're dealing with the school and the student disappears for two days and they do something else and they come back here and the students themselves say that they find it very different, that the university seems more theoretical, abstract and rather remote. School, obviously, is the everyday practice and there are all kinds of immediate pressures that they have to deal with. I tend to leave the philosophy in a sense out and tend to concentrate on this worked, this didn't work, what can we learn about your relationship and so on, what about the variety of approaches you can take, and by so doing take the philosophy as read. (English mentor, male, Head of Department)

The long-standing tensions about coverage that exist in HEI and school partnerships are once again highlighted: the perceived theory–practice divide which traditionally characterised many teacher training courses is still apparent. And yet according to this mentor at least, a student must possess certain beliefs about the subject, beliefs which are acted out in the way the student teaches, manages the classroom and establishes relationships with pupils.

> You know in a sense the philosophy comes out in what they are doing, you know their teaching strategy and their classroom management and their relationship with pupils. You can see to some extent obviously their beliefs.

They must have those beliefs. (English mentor, male, Head of Department)

It is by these practices that the student teacher is assessed. So, although 'philosophy' as this mentor puts it, is not the subject for discussion in mentor sessions, it is nevertheless what makes students function in the way that they do in any classroom and is therefore a fundamental part of the basis for judgements of competence: an important aspect of trainee assessment remains a matter of tacit judgement.

English: how can different beliefs be identified?

In an initial interview, this mentor reiterates the importance of beliefs:

> You know I always say to A-level students: you're not here to read books, you're here to find out how your heart works – and obviously that sounds rather odd to them because I'm talking about your feelings and yourself as a person and books are a way into that rather than some kind of object. (English mentor, male, Head of Department)

These interesting comments reveal a particular Leavisite attitude to the teaching of English. One may usefully compare them with comments made by a male lecturer quoted in *English People* (Evans 1993:131),

> The Leavisite view, then, can be put very simply: 'I see it as a subject about how we live, how we are to live'. 'The question was, what does it mean to be human – the meaning of existence. You were given the answer at the same time, to be human is to study English Literature.'

English teachers who adopt a Leavisite approach to their teaching would be characterised as emphasising the following: close reading focusing on plot, character, and so on, as a core skill and thus privileging the text itself over knowledge about the text or the author; close reading designed to confirm the value of an already valued text; sensitivity to the beauty of the text which provokes an emotional response; and recognising that the close reading aims to make an objective statement both about the text and about the subjective response.

A case study

In the transcript of one particular mentor session some very interesting dialogue occurs. Here, the differences in the mentor's and student's underlying beliefs about English teaching are revealed in their discussion about classroom experiences. (Italics are ours and indicate evidence of the mentor's beliefs informing classroom practice.) The discussion opens with the mentor talking about his way of teaching poetry.

M: It was actually a cloze exercise of a Ted Hughes poem and then they had to consider the effects of the words. Firstly, obviously they had to work out why this word fitted and why not the other one and then *consider the effect the words have.* And I wonder if you could tie that in? *What effect* ... OK they've recognised it, they've seen the link between the visual and the written ... *Why's this description a better one than the other one?* What gave us the clue for linking this tree to that? Does it tell us anything about the writer's view of nature ? Or anything about the trees themselves ? So they're actually focusing on the diction ... the primary question is language is complex, especially poetry. *Why does a writer choose particular words? What effect* ... or one way to say what associations does that word have that this other word doesn't? So you can easily contrast one or two of the images ... they will hopefully recognise *the term imagery* ... *say which do you think is a better one?* And again you can link that in to the work they've been doing in *Which struck you as the best? Why?* Preparation for the unseen poem in the exam. You know on a very pragmatic note that is their first exam ... the unseen poem ... that's the one they find hardest... what they find hardest is dealing with the language ... finding anything to say about it other than the literal: this is what happens in the poem. *And it's trying to push them beyond that into commenting on it's [the language's] effect. How does it work? What does it make you think of? Or what does it make you feel?*

So, if you think after the recognition if you like that they then have to choose something after that ... or give them another poem where they've got to pick out the images ... see if they can recognise the images and the description. *And they've actually got to comment specifically.... give them that fixed task, say six words or phrases and tell me what effect* ... Or you could even get them to write down the connotations of that word ... what does it make you think of? What's in the actual poem on the trees? *What words could we use? You could use that as an example* ... *Have they got anything like 'stiff', 'upright' 'towering'?* [Trainee hands mentor some examples] *These are good* ... *'clouds', 'veil', 'blackthreads' 'naked' 'stabbing' and 'flaring' they're all very good for words ... with onomatopoeic effects and for connotations.* You might want to do it with that before you go on to another one, or you may just want to stay with that.

S: I thought I could look at this and then at the structure of the poem itself. They could write their own.
(male mentor, English, Head of Department, and male trainee)

The mentor is encouraging the student to engage a class in ways which are explicitly Leavisite: a poem is provided, the author given, and discussion and close reading confirm why this already valued text is a valued text. This mentor expects pupils to begin to look closely at the language of the poem and have a feeling response however difficult it is for them to do. *Or what does it make you feel?* This is what Eagleton wittily refers to as the wine-tasting school of criticism. 'Sniff. Oh this has a fine, nutty flavour' (1983:134). More recent literary theorists have opposed this kind of criticism which made confident judgements without explicit criteria. It is clear that the student teacher wishes to engage in a debate about English teaching that moves it away from the mentor's Leavisite stance. The student continues the discussion about teaching poetry. He feels the lesson was exciting because a pupil has rejected the accepted approach to the poem.

S: I had my first Friday afternoon last Friday as well ... with a class. They're nice ... but even they were quite rowdy.

M: Were they?

S: Not rowdy, but excitable ... they all wanted attention and they all had things to say .... But it was probably the most intellectual stimulation I've had since I've been here with this class because we were doing this poem 'The Trees in Winter' or rather 'The Winter Trees' and we were looking at imagery in that poem. One of the lines is 'A shadow bends and picks up a cigarette end'. And I asked them 'Who's the shadow?' expecting 'Oh it's a man he's poor, he's a tramp'. And some of them came out with that. That's what I expected really. Now there's that image and it's associated with a winter tree ... barren ... alone. And I said 'Is there any connection here? Is the poet trying to make any connection between these two?' And one boy said to me 'Well how do you know it's a man?' I said 'I don't know, does it say he's a man?' 'No, it doesn't sir, how can you say he's a man.' 'Good, how do you know he's poor?' Somebody else said 'Well he's picking up a cigarette end. Why else would he do it?' 'That doesn't mean he's poor, sir.'

M: Keep Britain Tidy

S: He'd done this work with X (another member of the department). He's black... The class had been doing some work on images of the Third World, and how often it sees these poor people ... rather paternal ... So he pipes up and is telling me *'Where's the evidence for this? How do you know this man is poor? How do you know he's unhappy? How can the poet say this?'*
   So I say 'That's a very fair point ... very true'. *And I was thinking in a sense that is part of what English is about really, that you get these... numerous readings of the same thing and often I find myself giving one and saying right that's that. And to actually find someone to actually say 'Well no'. That's really good.*

M: 'It's good if they can challenge you. Usually, of course teachers are ready to give their prepared reading.

S: Yeah. *He's an intelligent lad. And he did it very cogently really... and kept asking me for evidence and I kept saying 'Well there's no evidence, other than the poem ok. So you can argue what you want from the poem as long as you use the poem... which he was... And I was saying I'm not having an argument with you. There isn't a right or wrong... which is another thing you rarely say... or rather I've rarely said.*

M: Well we're running out of time so if we just stop there and carry on this afternoon.

S: OK.

(They do not return to this subject during the session.)

The student is explicit in this dialogue about his own beliefs about English teaching; they are quite different to the mentor's. He seems to be seeking wider discussion about philosophies for English teaching. *And I was thinking in a sense that is part of what English is about really, that you get these ... numerous readings of the same thing and often I find myself giving one and saying right that's that. And to actually find someone to actually say 'Well no'. That's really good.* The mentor makes an appropriate response though he does not engage with the student's assertions about English teaching which, as represented here, are quite different from his own. The opportunity for discussion about subject beliefs is not taken up. Consequently, opportunity for stimulating engagement about what teachers are trying to do when they adopt specific strategies for teaching poetry is lost.

Other responses

It is possible to see how another mentor interviewed also initially responded with a Leavisite emphasis.

> But I suppose the bottom line for me, because we are a literature based department and I've always chosen to work in literature orientated departments, was a *sensitivity to literature* and a deep understanding of that, and it's, you know the things that go into making a work of literature, and the *ability to recognise and separate out those component parts, like character and plot, and above all a sort of sensitivity to language, particularly when you're dealing with poetry.* [authors' emphases]

However, this mentor was also aware of the problematic nature of defining English, and was cognisant of recent developments in English teaching.

> There's the whole National Curriculum debate anyway about what is the canon and what is of value, and it's a big crisis in English studies anyway, not just in schools, but at university level. What do you teach? What is a text? I mean for me it's not a debate I've ever resolved. Why do you think Shakespeare is better than, I don't know, Catherine Cookson or whatever, but you know ... I would say that that's my main aim ... stimulating a sort of love of literature. But also,

I mean, one of the problems with English is that you can see it in so many ways.... and use it as a study skills type subject, and so there's more of an emphasis on that.
(English mentor, female, not Head of Department)

Another mentor who also emphasised the importance of a love of literature, articulated her beliefs in the following way:

I think it helps you to be aware and sensitive, but I also think it helps you to perceive what is happening in the world around you. I think the study of literature is deeply political... So I think it is to do with sensitivity and growth, but also to do with looking at the way we organise things politically, and being able to comment critically... I think that's the skills that I would really want to bring out, does that sort of make sense?... I do think it's important to look at a variety of texts... I believe you do need your cultural background. So I'm not one of these people who say forget all your 'great' white European male writers... I would say let's add to them. You know the great white women writers, the great black women writers, and let's have something from the thirties, the seventies, the nineties... because they've all got statements to make in a way about what's important in our lives.
(English mentor, female, Head of Department)

The crisis in English teaching at university level identified by the previous mentor is also illustrated in these comments, though definitions of what English literature teaching involves were different for each respondent. Comparable differences were also revealed in other comments made during our interviews. It is not surprising that the wider debate about English is reflected in the range of perspectives that school teachers of English hold. What is surprising is that through lack of time, or uncertainty about the division of labour between the HEIs and schools and the changing role of the mentor, discussion with the student teachers about these beliefs seems at best minimal and at worst non-existent. And, more importantly, there is little done to enable the student or mentor to see that implicit beliefs may be influencing the overall judgement about the student's competence. This potential source of bias may not be so obvious if both appear to share the same approaches, but problems are likely to arise when they do not. How does this discrepancy of views influence the kind of training that takes place, especially if the student arrives, as in the case study already considered, with a cultural studies background and has to work with a mentor whose pedagogy seems rooted in a Leavisite approach? If the mentor's beliefs and those of the student remain tacit, the scope for real dialogue about practice may be very limited. Significantly, the divergence may contribute to a negative assessment of the student, and perhaps even result in the student's failure. The nature of the power relationship (Dart and Drake, 1993) may indeed prevent some students from trying to discuss such sensitive areas. Or the mentor may dismiss such attempts with easy assumptions about the students' lack of experience, their naïve enthusiasm about 'things they tell you in college, which don't really work at the chalk-face'. This tendency not to make underlying subject beliefs explicit was also found in mathematics.

Mathematics

Sanders (1994) argues that the applications of different mathematical philosophies to learning influences how classroom activities are interpreted. She suggests that among mathematics teachers, some 'were indicating that they felt mathematics is about remembering methods that other people have developed', whilst she herself believed it to 'include creativity and intuition and wanted to demonstrate to the pupils that they could be involved in developing methods as well'. She records that these differing beliefs produced an impasse in working relationships. Sanders also usefully recognises that teachers often assume that the same terms mean exactly the same thing to each person using them. The reality is clearly more complicated: 'group work', for example, actually covered a wide range of practices, all of which are described by the same term. As Sanders records, her attempts to clarify value stances resulted in a breakdown of working relationships, something that the student, as opposed to an already qualified and experienced teacher, is very careful to avoid. We would contend that student teachers have too much at stake to threaten the mentor–student relationship; they are rarely able to challenge a mentor, and indeed are under considerable pressure to emulate the mentor's practices and demonstrate that they hold a similar belief system, whether or not that is really the case. It is not always easy for the student to do this, for at least two reasons. First, they will to a large extent need to surmise what the mentor's beliefs about the subject are; as already noted, these may not at any time be made explicit. Second, if there is a clash in underlying beliefs students may find it difficult to make sense of practices emanating from a different belief system and therefore to emulate them. It is rare that either party sees the mentor–student relationship as an opportunity for debate about these beliefs. However, there may well be occasions when such tensions emerge. Our research illustrated these emerging tensions in the mentor–student dialogues which were a reflection of underlying beliefs about mathematics teaching.

Many new entrants to mathematics teaching will be immediately confronted by changes in pedagogy since they themselves were taught mathematics; the most significant one, as Cooper (1990) illustrates, is investigational mathematics. He points to specific anxieties on the part of PGCE students in this particular area, which at the time of writing has maintained its place in the Mathematics National Curriculum in the shape of Attainment Target One: Using and Applying Mathematics. Such anxieties are consistent with the lack of experience of novice teachers in doing investigational work at school themselves, and the inaccessibility of the practice of their experienced colleagues in school. An experienced mentor expressed it like this,

> Solving investigative ideas that are prevalent in maths classrooms which certainly weren't there ten or fifteen, perhaps twenty years ago ... certainly not in my experience. That can be quite difficult and I think that the mentor, and obviously the university, both have their role to play there if you like in bringing the student up-to-date with the curriculum content and the ideas behind it ... A student coming in who went through a very traditional schooling may find this sort of thing quite daunting.
> (mathematics mentor, male, not Head of Department)

Another identified the same phenomenon.

> The chances are at the moment that most people came through a far more traditional system certainly in maths teaching than we're offering at the moment. So it's unusual for them to think of the teacher not being at the front of the classroom with his piece of chalk in his hand saying this is how you do it kids. Now here's a book and there's ten million more to do just like that one and get on with it, because that's the sort of experience even young people, people in their twenties, will have had at school. Certainly people older than their twenties definitely will have had at school.
> (mathematics mentor, male, Head of Department)

Although mathematics mentors were able to articulate these changes in pedagogy, the different approaches they brought with them still created difficulties for students about when best to use an investigative strategy and when it would be better to use more traditional methods. For example, in the dialogue that follows, a student is confident about a LOGO lesson that he has just taught. However, the mentor who is also assisting in the lesson is less happy with what the pupils have actually learnt. The student explains his sense of the lesson's outcomes; he felt a conflict between adopting an investigative approach and relying on a more traditional didactic one.

M: Having done the construction poster they would know how to construct a polygon, and they would know something about the internal angles ... a lot about the internal angles really, the internal angles of a hexagon and perhaps the octagon. They'd figure that out. But it's quite a big jump for them to go from that to a new activity, you've almost got to connect it up for them. They don't transfer these skills very readily.

S: No, they don't, they don't seem to. They seem to have very short memories. But I was sort of trying to do it a bit investigationally so I wanted to try and encourage them to do one thing and if it wasn't right, to try again and try again until they'd kind of sussed out what it was. That is what I wanted, that was my main aim if you like. Having said that, if I'd gone with my heart if you like, if I'd followed the way that I would possibly feel more comfortable, I would have done a more formal lesson on shape geometry first, so that I would have been sure that when they went into the computer room they would know about shapes ... Or just first firmed up their knowledge, the fact that for a straight line the angle is 180 degrees. So they could perhaps work out those things.

M: You might be right on that, although, of course, there would be groups of them that wouldn't gather that.

Although the different ways of teaching are at least acknowledged here, reasons which may inform the use of either approach in this context remain implicit. More explicit discussion about these different methods would, we suggest, be desirable for the student's professional development.

In the extract that follows the mentor does attempt to discuss some assumptions about mathematics teaching, notably the tension that exists between classroom mathematics and mathematics in the real world. The prevailing culture in school mathematics is one which provides answers. In the real world this may often not be the case. Although the mentor provides opportunity for discussion about this, the student does not take it up.

M: So what sort of things when you're planning a day trip, exactly are the concerns, what are the main things they are actually looking at?

S: Well they're looking at time, they're looking for train schedules or bus schedules, they're going to be making the decision and I don't know yet if I should let them have a certain amount of imaginary money to spend. Do you think it would be a good idea ?

M: Yes, I don't see why not. If they have to cost it then they can see if it's feasible. One of the quite interesting things about something like that is that it brings home to the students perhaps a lot of problems that they solve in the maths classroom are in some ways quite artificial. Often, but not always, there may well be a solution. Whereas with a problem like that quite often there are inconsistencies and there are trade-offs that have to be made. For instance, if you're going to travel to a certain place it may be that travelling by one mode of transport will be cheaper than travelling by another, but you will get there a lot later and so students have got to sort that problem, about how important it is, you know is money more important than time? You know, I save money but get there two hours late. So these sort of decisions are quite involved when you think about the kinds of problems people solve in their day-to-day life. It brings home a different flavour, certainly to the text book approach of here's ten questions and, normally,there's a right answer. There isn't a right answer to questions like that. And they are difficult things to resolve.

Sometimes the answer is made for you, because for instance if you're going to a show and it starts at a certain time and you've no option if you're going to get there.

S: I think there's lots of different things for them to look at, a lot of decisions to make, should they bring their lunch, should they buy their lunch, should they buy a travel card for the tube, are they going to have to call home, will they want to buy a souvenir. I'm sure that they will come up with many more ideas than I have right now.

(mathematics mentor, male, Head of Department and mathematics student teacher, female)

The possibility here for discussion about different ways of perceiving mathematics teaching is lost. The student's response to the mentor's introduction of real world mathematics, as opposed to classroom learning, is merely an answer to her own question about what they might need an imaginary amount of money for. It does not embrace the wider philosophy that the mentor has outlined. As Sanders (1994:34) writes,

> Once such differing views of Mathematics are recognised it seems clear that they need to be articulated in order for teachers to work together. It is not sufficient for teachers to assume they share a common view. In the relationship between a mentor and student teacher, it must be important for the mentor to ensure that perspectives are discussed.

Sanders proposes that mentors early on in their relationship with trainees address the following questions:

- What is mathematics ?
- What does it mean to learn mathematics ?
- What does it mean to teach mathematics ?

Such discussion in any subject is vital. An understanding of different perspectives will be central to the trainees' ability to engage in reflective practice. Once the implicit beliefs and values of any subject are made explicit and discussed there may be several other positive outcomes: the conflict that might emerge in the student–mentor relationship may be prevented; both student and mentor will approach the statements of competence from a mutual understanding about the complexities underlying them; and the opportunities for dynamic and reflective practice are likely to be increased.

Some conclusions

How, then, do 'Subject Knowledge' and 'Subject Application' compe-tences relate to mentors' repeated claims of seeking someone who first and foremost possesses 'a love of literature'?

I think it is somebody who, who is really interested in texts and can actually

convey that enthusiasm for the written material to pupils, and also in terms of writing as well, *a real genuine love of literature.*
(English mentor, female, Head of Department)

So a good English teacher has got to be able to enjoy reading and be able to communicate *not only a love of literature* but knowledge about how certain aspects and qualities of that literature have been achieved.
(English mentor, female, Head of Department)

Obviously a love of subject and *a love of literature in particular.*
(English mentor, male, Head of Department)

How are the competences to be interpreted by mathematics mentors who, on the other hand, were aware of the tensions they felt between wanting well-qualified mathematicians and those who would facilitate children's learning? These two qualities did not always seem to go together. The fast pace of change in education meant that for mathematics mentors, in particular, students' ability to learn and adapt was given considerable emphasis as qualities necessary for competence. The need was for

Someone who is very flexible and who's prepared to go along with the enormous changes that have been imposed on Mathematics teachers over the last five or six years.
(mathematics mentor, male, not Head of Department)

It is clear from our research that a student teacher has to gain a good understanding of the subject's culture and status within a school as well as any hidden expectations that mentors may be seeking when they assess competence. We suggest that those involved in the training process often appear to have very different interpretations of these competence statements, based on their institutional as well as their individual practices, beliefs and values. Inevitably, subject ideologies inform all professional conduct, permeate mentors' work with their students and form the basis for their judgement on student competence. Student teachers, in response, need quickly to comprehend the complexities of school and subject culture through which the generalised statements of competence are interpreted, as well as to make sense of them in the light of their existing knowledge and experience. Students as well as mentors interpret competence statements in the light of their own philosophies.

Some of these subject-specific concerns arise from issues of knowledge and understanding as they are currently written in the 'Subject Knowledge' and 'Subject Application' statements of competence. Many reasons might be given to explain why a competence-based model of assessment for teacher training has been recently implemented by the government: to improve standards in England and Wales by applying a common set of competences to training wherever and however it might take place; to begin a process that is intended to sustain career-long professional development; to ensure the continuation of the Government's interventionist and controlling role in what is taught. The first reason is based on the assumption that the preferred model of assessment of newly qualified teachers is, by virtue of clear statements of areas of competence, relatively unproblematic. However, as Argyris and Schön (1974) argue, making implicit 'theories in use' explicit and thereby open to criticism is the key to professional learning. The scheduled mentor session coupled with the increase in the time students spend in school provides a significant opportunity for this kind of professional learning to occur. It is therefore incumbent on mentor and student alike to persevere with making all the implicit aspects of practice explicit. The implications for partnership practices are clear: are there ways that the university can, in conjunction with schools, prepare student teachers to think about the underlying beliefs of their subject and enable them to see their influence in the teaching of it? The challenge for all those involved, in HEIs as well as in schools, is how best to achieve this within the changing partnership arrangements.

Acknowledgements

We are indebted to Tony Becher for all his help and encouragement. We would also like to thank the teachers involved in the project: Chris Anderson, Alison Browning, Krys Buleska, Adrian Burnett, Elaine Comski, Rowland Darby, Teresa Dickens, Ella Dzelzanis, John Heaton, Adrian Hinckley, Wayne Jones, Ken Leonard, Liz Lockwood, Deidra McCloughlin, Uday Patel, Keith Perara, Eddie Slater, Sarah Smith and Gill Weinrib.

Notes

1. Trainees have one hour a week timetabled to meet with their mentor. Discussion covers all aspects of their continuing professional development.
2. At the time of the research, March 1994, there were five attainment targets in mathematics. At the time of writing, December 1994, further reorganisation of mathematics in the National Curriculum has resulted in four attainment targets for children entering Key Stages 3 and 4 in September 1995, and three attainment targets for children entering Key Stage 1.

CHAPTER 5

Issues in the Management of Mentoring

Derek Glover and George Mardle

The organisational framework

This report is concerned with the way in which mentoring is arranged within the schools. Keele has had a partnership arrangement with about thirty schools for the past three years and it was becoming clear following student evaluation that there was a great deal of variation in the way the schools in the partnership managed student involvement. At a philosophical level, schools are having to adapt to their new responsibilities, and there are great variations in the ways in which they view the opportunities provided by the new situation and in their interpretation of the rationale for involvement. The collective 'school' is endowing the institution with a common view that is not substantiated in practice – frequently we believed the decision-making to have been undertaken by a small management committee, or indeed, the head alone, without open discussion with the staff as a whole. The philosophical view of the partnership leads to an interpretation of the redistribution of financial payments which results in an enormous variation in transfer payments of time or money to mentors, in the use of resources for the benefit of the whole school, and in the integration of mentoring arrangements with other aspects of school organisation. This has led to variation in attitudes to the selection, training, roles and support for professional and subject mentors. The impact of the new arrangements on all elements of the school community – pupils, other staff, parents and in some schools, governors, affects attitudes.

Our contention is that where these attitudes are positive, and where there is a common view of the mutual benefits of partnership involvement, the student gains a great deal. Where there is no common sense of purpose, where the activity is bolted on to existing arrangements, and where the students are seen as a source of additional income rather than as a contribution to total professional development, the student may suffer a negative experience. We return to this theme in the conclusion to our report after examining the issues arising from the varied management arrangements for mentoring.

Our evidence comes from questionnaire responses by 100 mentors in the Keele partnership schools and qualitative data from 20 case study schools investigated to a common format by a field worker and a team of five practising mentors. The format for the semi-structured interviews was agreed by the participating mentors. The field notes and case study notes were then written to provide data on both individual and organisational involvement in mentoring and the impact of change upon the organisation of each school. Ten of the case study schools were from the Keele partnership, and five each from partnerships with Worcester College of Higher Education and the University College of St. Martin, Lancaster. As the majority practice has been to call school subject staff 'mentors', with organisation and liaison undertaken by a professional mentor, and HEI subject staff 'tutors', with liaison as the responsibility of a curriculum or link tutor, these conventions will be followed in the report. To avoid confusion the teachers in training will be referred to as associate teachers, or ATs.

The three HEIs have all established a contract with their partnership schools over the last three years. As a consequence there is an expectation on the part of the HEI that mentoring will provide a substantial element of the teacher education process according to the guidelines and mentor training developed by the HEI. In each partnership the contract was offered to participating schools when they were asked to undertake enhanced training work and includes items such as the provision of teaching opportunities for the student, assessment and reporting, and participation in professional development as part of whole school experience. Guidelines, evolved by the professional studies staff of the HEI in co-operation with representative staff of the schools, then extend the contract in a practical way by linking the work of the HEI to the anticipated experiences at subject and whole school level. As an example, the subject guidelines of one HEI ask that the schools provide an opportunity for associates to experience individual, group and whole class work in the the use of language in English teaching. It is recognised that whilst we were working with schools from three different partnerships there was a commonality of philosophy and practice which allowed us to make assertions about the nature of mentoring and its impact.

Origin and impetus

The concern in this part of the investigation was to see how the newer patterns of partnership were evolving to meet the requirement that at least 66% of initial teacher training be school-based. This involved the school staff in the management of change as they undertook to have more students within the schools for a longer period each year. They were also faced with the adaptation of existing practices to meet the increased time and training demands on supervising staff as they became more responsible for the induction, competence development, professional growth, assessment and pastoral development of associate teachers. The research showed that in virtually all aspects of policy development and practice organisation there is a spectrum of practice which might be seen as the difference between the 'bolt on' and the integrated view of initial teacher training as a school responsibility.

In six of the case study schools the first move towards acceptance of a contractual arrangement offered by the HEI was made by the head. Motivation for involvement appeared to exist at three levels. At its lowest there was a wish to be at the forefront of new developments which might bring a continuing, and possibly stronger link with the HEI 'for curriculum purposes in the main where it helps if we know who to talk to'. Awareness of external relations has led some schools to capitalise on the involvement in an attempt to enhance the reputation of the school with parents and governors in the belief that participation was a reflection of perceived quality. At the highest level heads admitted that participation might bring opportunities for school improvement through staff involvement in training. Three of the schools where the head was prime mover, and a further five where the impetus came from elsewhere, had had a long association with the HEI concerned and saw the move towards a contractual relationship as a natural progression which could be achieved without major change. However, there is a clear difference between those schools where the change was made on the assumption that staff would agree to greater participation and those where there was a longer period of negotiation. One school comments that

> despite the previous involvement we were aware that strong unionisation and awareness of the increased workload meant that we could only go along with the plan if the staff as a whole were willing.

In a further six schools the impetus for participation came from a member of the senior management team, usually the deputy who had previously undertaken the liaison with the HEI, but the approaches to staff were made in different ways. In one school the mentors 'were identified because the senior management team knew the qualities they were looking for', in three the departments were told of the scheme on offer and asked to volunteer, and in four schools the case for participation was outlined to the staff as a whole by a member of the senior management team after negotiation with the HEI staff.

> At no time was any great importance attached to the fact that the school would be paid for the involvement – it was sold on what it could do for staff as a pilot at the forefront of developments .

In two schools the prime movers were other than members of the senior management team but they appear to have developed their interest because of links with the HEI. The introduction of the new scheme appears to have been with the agreement of unions in eleven of the schools, and with the approval of governors in seven. The responses from the former indicated that the involvement should be on a voluntary basis and there is evidence that union representatives in five schools rejected any payment to mentors at this stage whilst those in three others were anxious to secure payment for the extra work undertaken. The governors have been involved where the 'change of policy was such that approval for the existing scheme could not be sufficient', and all approved participation, although two reservations were expressed 'that it should not be detrimental to the progress of the pupils' and 'that it should be reviewed if the workload for the staff appeared to be too great'. In two schools the views of parents were sought and there was no dissent.

Introducing change

Whilst the origin and impetus for participation in the contractual arrangements came mainly from the head or senior management there are clear examples of evolution and revolution at work in the establishment of organisational practice. The continuum here is from the unplanned and piecemeal approach seen at one extreme where 'there was an assumption that the system would evolve as we attempted to meet the new demands of the HEI', to the planned whole school approach where a new scheme was started from scratch. This was exemplified where the decision to take up to eleven associates was seen as part of a total revision of professional development policy reviewed by members of departments, individual teaching and ancillary staff, and governors.

Evolution is a process of adaptation 'where the way in which we have worked with associates in the past has been changed as we have coped with new administrative and assessment methods', and where 'we have well-established patterns within departments and have modified these to cope with what the HEI wants'. It does, however, bring with it new features – principally the need to determine the distribution of resources, especially where payment to mentors is concerned, but also the establishment of new staff relationships as where 'the mentors for their part see themselves very much as a team whose views are sought on the management of the scheme'. Schools have realised the need to develop these teams with the professional mentor to secure coherence and uniformity of approach but appear to have been slower to recognise the structural implications of any organisational change.

Revolution appears to have occurred in those schools which have changed arrangements on a large scale. One case study school had had no teachers in training for four years but agreed to take ten in the first term of the new arrangements. A professional mentor had been appointed to undertake the work, mentors appointed and a mentoring system put in place as part of the added responsibility of the senior teacher for professional development. At another a similar number of associate teachers were introduced after agreement with two HEIs for involvement on a quid pro quo arrangement which was acceptable to staff because of the offer of widespread accredited training, and a belief that major curriculum changes could be achieved with the additional classroom support believed to be available during the training period. In each case major policy documents were prepared, all stakeholders were consulted and the governors were involved.

Resource allocation

Whilst the contractual agreement between HEIs and the schools specifies the payment of a per capita fee for each student trained this is no guarantee that the resources will be transferred in such a way that the mentor is paid for the additional work undertaken. The questionnaire responses indicate that 49% of mentors are paid for their work, 21% are given time to undertake the duties, 31% are guaranteed non-contact time, and 8% are allocated both time and payment. Of the twenty case study schools only seven return a significant proportion of the fee to the mentoring staff, eight have a system of varying complexity which returns some payment or time in lieu to mentoring departments, and the remaining five use the resources for departmental or whole school benefit but with no personal payment for mentoring duties.

Where the resources are paid to the mentors, in three cases with appropriate job descriptions and agreements, the payment ranges from £320 to £1,000 per mentor. The remaining money is then distributed to school, department and associate resource headings. In one school which has been evolving a scheme which meets the needs of professional development the payment is converted to time and each mentor is allocated two lessons each week but also receives some 'college training credit' for personal professional development. As in three of the 'direct payment' schools the residue of the fee income is paid to the professional mentor. In one school with a long association with the HEI an attempt has been made to cost the activity with the notional timing of hours of contact per term used as part of the formula which gives 15% of the income to a central fund 'which becomes part of the undetermined pot for school benefit', pays for the additional involvement of the professional mentor in assessment and administration, and then allocates an hourly payment for five hours in the first term, eleven hours in the main block practice and five hours in the summer term.

Where payments are made indirectly, that is within the school but not to the mentors, the schools have a formula which attempts to balance the varying additional time and resource demands consequent upon a revised mentoring procedure. These arrangements are illustrated in one school where the fees support a time allocation to the deputy head (as professional mentor), £123 per subject department involved for additional books and materials needed, and £500 to each head of department to deploy as the department agrees for mentor supervision.

Although the evidence of ill-feeling caused by payment systems is limited there are clearly situations where tensions have developed.

> There is no value given to mentoring in my school and hence no money or set time for mentors … the only person who gets most of the benefit is the so-called professional mentor, and as long as she gets her money and time, the rest do not matter at all.

Feelings are also occasionally directed against the school.

> At the end of the exercise and not being too cynical, there are bonuses for the school in being involved – money being the big one. If you provide a starving donkey with a carrot then you can only expect it to eat it … I am gravely concerned when the aim of the professional mentor is to get more associates into the school.

In those schools which do not make any personal payment to mentors this appears to be on the basis that it is morally wrong to single out staff in this way, or because the practicalities of organisation inhibit such a move. Some respondents sought to remove any possible cause of tension within the staffroom in the belief that 'mentoring relies on goodwill, if you start paying for it you change the emphasis totally and this could be a cause of tension'. In all except one of the case study schools where there has been some comment on the decision not to make payments to mentors this is attributed to the head, for example as 'the head is opposed to the idea of payment and no payment is ever likely to be made to mentors', but there is evidence of a contrary shift of staff opinion and some departments have agreed to pay mentors from devolved funds in recognition of their additional duties. Where the decision not to pay was taken because 'we as a staff felt that there was so much whole school involvement in the training and we wanted the money to help us all', the funding is split four ways between professional mentor time, INSET opportunities for mentoring staff, improvements to benefit the associates (this year by refurbishing a work base), and departmental resources.

Evidence of recent change suggests that schools which have not previously made direct payments to mentors are beginning to do so 'in response to the increase in moneys into school from the partnership and in recognition of the increase in work associated with mentoring'. Whilst this is the only school which appears to have recognised an increase in funding, it is one of four which have been able to devise a scheme of payment which meets the demands for flexibility of mentoring contact, possibly by different staff, throughout the school year, and it reflects the move towards some recompense for the additional work 'which is not what we would always have done but the extra which arises from developing a new scheme within the schools'.

Time management

Some additional time allocation is used as an alternative to direct payment in some schools. Eight of the professional mentors have an allocation of time, six in lieu of the fact that they are not paid a supplement for their work, and two because this is regarded as an additional responsibility. Four schools make a specific time allocation varying from two periods per associate mentored, described as 'sufficient for the extra paper-work', to one lesson of guaranteed protected time free from cover duties which is 'valued by the mentors but is seen as only a small part of the overall time given to associates'.

The other sixteen schools make a variety of arrangements which show the differing philosophies behind senior management views of mentoring. The more extreme views may be seen in accounts of eight schools where, for example, 'the mentors are getting paid in lieu of time', 'the load is to be carried along with the function', and 'no time is allocated because this is work to be undertaken out of school except for the professional mentor who has an additional administrative burden'. In the other eight schools there is a more sensitive recognition that the time allocation may 'not be practicable because of the varying demands across the year and the late notification of the associates and their programme', and 'the need for the coincidence of free time'. Even here there is evidence of compromise arrangements, for example where the senior management felt that

> although there was pressure on mentors to give time over and above what is necessary in the early part of the year there would be gains for them at the end of the year with associates taking on more of the lessons of mentors ... and arrangements would be made for cover at particular times when mentors need it.

Management structures

The introduction of a major responsibility has had management implications in all schools although three of the twenty schools convey the impression that mentoring is a 'bolt on' to normal administration. In only two schools the management is concentrated in the hands of a head or deputy where 'the head makes the key decisions because he carries the final contractual responsibility and because he works with the deputy head as professional mentor', and where 'the system is controlled by the deputy head as professional mentor with a clear link to the head who sees the system as a reaction to ·immediate needs rather than as part of permanent policy'. In both schools the degree of other senior staff involvement appears to be limited.

In ten schools the professional mentor is a member of the senior management team and as such is able to influence policy within the existing format. This may convey an impression of central administration and policy determination where 'there is a clear feeling that the whole scheme is centrally controlled and mentor input is peripheral to the making of policy', but the 'ease of decision making and the flexibility has been fundamental to the development of a scheme which looks after eleven associates each year' is recognised in another school.

All the remaining schools have the professional mentor following a delegated role which is more or less an administrative one according to the philosophy, time available and previous practice of the staff concerned. Relationships and consultative processes vary from school to school but those schools which have a downward delegated professional mentor appear to have more strongly developed mentoring teams. In the five schools where the professional mentor role is undertaken by a deputy head there is a tendency for the management of the associates to be more firmly placed in the hands of the mentors and this can lead to a lack of coherence where there are no formal structures for planning, co-ordination and the development of common policies in matters of assessment.

The integration of initial teacher education and the school development planning process provides some indication of the structural changes within school management. In eight of the case study schools the initial teacher training work is recognised as part of the School Development Plan – a sign that the commitment is recognised as being relatively long term and with staffing and resource implications. It is significant that three of the four schools associated with HEIs which offer some accreditation for mentoring are included within the group which have an emphasis on departmental planning

In only five schools has the work become integrated with other aspects of professional development policy including INSET and appraisal but where this has been introduced staff have become aware of the benefits of the flexibility and the increase in training opportunities for all staff not just the mentors. Our evidence suggests that this may be a second stage of development requiring more time and confidence in operation before the senior staff of schools wish to

> convey the view that we are irretrievably committed to something about which we have serious doubts with the present funding.
>
> (Deputy Head, professional mentor)

The nature of involvement

Most schools have sought a voluntary element in the appointment of mentors. From the case studies it would seem that 58 mentors out of a possible 85 felt that they had volunteered for the role but this had been in response to open advertisement in three schools only.

A more general method is for the heads of department to be faced with the recruitment of mentors because of an agreement to participate. The 'number of people from whom they can choose is very small, it is usually a job which has to be done and which can only be done by the number two because he or she has the length of experience it needs'. This appears to have happened in eight schools but practice varies and some of these have no volunteers because the head of department has undertaken the role.

If negotiation within the department might have minimised tension, direct approaches from the professional mentor which have occurred in five schools could actually exacerbate problems where 'the professional mentor approaches individual staff and asks for their co-operation before talking matters over with the head of department'.

The criteria for selection, either by invitation or by internal advertisement response, include 'some experience of teacher training', 'former involvement with the HEI scheme', ' a long period of successful teaching', 'the skills of empathy, supporting and counselling', 'an ability to cope with the administrative work and the integration of associates with the life of the school', 'an awareness of the way in which the subject should be developing' and 'a genuine interest in the work'. Job descriptions are used in connection with the role in five schools and are part of the appraisal process in two of these. Mentors generally feel that 'the work might be of use for the c.v.', 'it provides an opportunity to focus reflection on our work', 'it might help when it comes to looking for another job', and 'it gives a strong interest to diversify the teaching pattern'. Whilst this would suggest that they do not rank the work highly in securing promotion, staff of the three schools linked to an accreditation scheme with their local HEI are on a waiting list for involvement in mentoring. Only three of the heads would look at former mentoring experience in seeking new appointments, and only one would advertise for staff with this experience.

The professional mentors appear to have been recruited either by designation by the head (seven schools), usually by the addition of the role to that of other work undertaken by deputy heads; appointed, usually by internal advertisement or approach to a senior teacher or head of faculty (nine schools); or inherited in so far as they had previously been the link for placements by the HEI.

Associates are aware of the pressures which mentoring brings and felt that heads of department were not always able to give the time required. They were similarly critical of deputy heads as professional mentors 'because they have other duties and see us as administrative work rather than as real people'.

Impact

The impact of the enlarged mentoring activity and the revised initial teacher education scheme

> put a heavy pressure on the schools which in the interest of the pupils, they may have to consider as an unwanted burden.
> (Head)

The management of reputation and the avoidance of unwanted parental criticism has affected the way in which the associates link into the school.

It would seem that there is a continuum of experience from the uncoordinated to the totally planned and the case studies although tending to the latter have provided evidence of some of the disruption which results. They speak of the 'time lost in the early days of a practice when we have to do so much to support the associate', 'impact of a large associate presence on a small school where the parents might complain at the way in which the normal teaching programme is disrupted', and 'coping with the problems which stem from those colleagues who are not involved but who are quick to point out problems which may arise from time to time'.

Where the picture is much more positive (in twelve of the schools) the benefits include 'the availability of additional staff in the classroom and in the school as a whole – it increases pupil support', 'the new ideas which are something for the regular staff to consider when they have time to reflect', 'the possibility of additional input for assessment, team teaching, project and individual work', 'the opportunity for departmental development with additional help', 'the avoidance of the disruptive impact of turning the students loose with a group', and 'the change from the student to the associate culture'. Schools also mention the involvement of associates in extra-mural activities, music, drama and personal and social education over a much longer period.

The schools which have planned their course in conjunction with the information from the HEIs appear to have developed a gentle induction into teaching in a way which minimises the problems of class management. The case studies show that seven schools maintain an audit of student exposure to classes and individuals. One school reports two parental adverse comments in a year, another three from parents and two from pupils, but by and large 'the associates do bring gains in enthusiasm, team teaching and in class support'. There are concerns, however, at the impact of ten associates in one school, eleven in another and eight in another.

The individual and the organisation

The mentors

Whilst the voluntary nature of recruitment is questioned the mentors generally agree that they undertook the work willingly 'in response to the opportunity to work alongside associates in the classroom', 'to gain something from their freshness and enthusiasm as we attempted to justify the way in which we did things', 'to discipline ourselves so that we looked at aspects of our own classroom management', and 'to become involved with the HEI who were able to give a broader perspective on what was happening in education'.

Monetary rewards or additional time allocation are not seen to influence willingness to mentor. 'The money I get to do the job is less than I pay the chap who comes to do the gardening so that I can do the work', and 'the amount of time that the process takes, especially with different associates in each term, is out of step with any time which I might be able to claim – I do the work because I enjoy working with young people and because we do get something from them as we work together'. Whilst the mentors appear to have been motivated by higher ideals, and the experience of associates generally shows that this has been so, there is evidence that the additional work is a burden for those professional mentors who have other heavy administrative roles.

There is a spread of teaching experience by staff acting as mentors, ranging from those with no previous experience to staff with 33 years of teaching, the median is 16 years service. This raises the issue of just how much experience is needed before a teacher has sufficient competence to mentor another, and indeed, whether some colleagues 'might be too set in their ways to be effective mentors'.

For the professional mentors there is perhaps more career advantage in that the involvement with staff development practices, the management of complex administrative arrangements and the development of personal and group relationships provides important evidence for future management potential. Five of the professional mentors see this as a way forward but three others, all deputy heads, indicate that they have found the new role to be motivating because it has brought a new interest at a low point in their career.

Role definition

The mentors have developed their own view of their role. This includes sole responsibility for induction (34%), giving information on classes (57%), providing a timetable (73%), and providing a weekly tutorial (70%). Joint responsibility with other staff, usually the professional mentor, is undertaken for assisting with a second subject (50%), provision of wider school involvement for the associate (60%), and for associate counselling (75%). The organisation to support this role includes daily contact with associates for 64% of the mentors, spending one to three hours per week in discussing work with associates by 86%, and attending formal meetings with associates on a weekly basis by 68% of the respondents. There is also a perceived obligation to attend mentor group meetings termly for 68% of mentors, although 22% do not have such meetings.

Schools have been aware of the change in procedures and have generally sought to evolve new approaches in accordance with the guidance given by the HEI. Staff in thirteen schools appear to think that the framework for operation has been determined by the HEI, four feel that there is a joint planning relationship and the remaining three feel that the HEI has limited influence because the department or the individual operate in their own way. The professional mentors realised that the guidelines were given to ensure a degree of uniformity in practice, in accordance with the expectations of the contractual arrangements but 'with the understanding that we would use the mentoring handbook with a degree of flexibility'.

The staff who tended to make most use of the guidelines were, however, aware of the need to reconcile the needs of the individual associate and the school situation. Interviews with the subject staff of one of the HEIs concerned suggest that there may be problems where traditional approaches to teacher training are maintained or where idiosyncratic mentors have been appointed.

Five of the twenty schools have some form of job description for mentors, evolved within the school and negotiated between the professional mentors and the mentors, either as a team, or individually. These job descriptions are built upon the contractual parameters, for example including reference to the completion of professional development profiles, but they also recognise that 'the role is neither permanent nor a key to future development within the school – it is a matter of an evolving situation within its context'.

Skill identification

Mentors were asked to assess their ability and experience for aspects of their work. In the elements of their role model over 75% believed that they had good pupil teacher relationships, the ability to identify and build on good practice, and good working relationships with colleagues; 73% employed a variety of teaching methods. However, there appears to be a need for help in matters of time organisation (where only 52% of respondents felt that they had the ability and experience), self evaluation skills (42%), support for management initiatives (54%), effective communication skills (62%) and good organisation and administration (61%).

In their counselling role the only element to score highly in ability and experience was in lesson planning (80%), and skills development needs were identified in supporting associates with personal difficulties, helping them to develop confidence, guiding them in job applications and representing associate interests to other staff. In monitoring and assessment mentors believed that they had experience and ability on a lower level especially in providing assessment information (38%), and assisting in the completion of personal profiles (32%). There was more confidence in lesson observation (68%) and giving feedback on lessons (62%), providing subject knowledge (72%), providing resource details (84%), and setting the work within the context of the school (70%).

The participants appear to have similar views of the skills needed for effective mentoring. These include 'the ability to listen, to empathise and support', 'basic counselling skills', 'knowledge of your subject and the way in which it can be taught most effectively', 'the ability to reflect on what is happening in a lesson', and 'thorough knowledge of observation, assessment and skills development strategies'.

Sixteen of the schools have mentors who see that the HEIs set the parameters for mentoring by the guidelines which are issued and the training which is provided. The mentors accept that there is a need for uniformity of practice, administration which fits in with the HEI and CATE (Council for Accreditation of Teacher Education) requirements, and a basic framework for the school experience throughout a year. In all these schools there is a feeling that training has been inadequate and that 'the school has had to develop skills-based training to supplement the HEI meetings'. The four schools involved in accreditation have identified skills through developmental training and the development of conceptual frameworks for associate learning and assessment.

Professional development

The opportunity for further professional development appears to be a recurrent motivating feature in those schools which are associated with HEIs which offer accreditation for their certificate in mentoring course. The lack of such stimulation is a cause for concern in the training experienced by other HEIs where there is 'a concern with the administration and not with the learning process'.

Twelve of the schools indicate that they are seeking a more conceptual approach to 'mentor education rather than training', and three schools indicate that they would prefer to have HEI staff help to devise their own schemes within the school context. The professional mentor in one school sees the need for 'something which is not so much training as the evolution of a way of working and an understanding of the way in which the learning process can be managed for whatever age'.

Career profiles

Whilst there does seem to be some progression from head of faculty to professional mentor, or some rearrangement of duties so that a deputy becomes involved in staff development work, there is no evidence of an emerging career profile for mentors.

Twelve of the case studies indicate that most of the mentors had arrived at their present situation in an unplanned way and on a purely opportunistic basis, and only three of the remaining schools suggest that their mentors may have a clear career path in which mentoring plays a part. The range of opinion may be seen in that one mentor comments that 'there is not yet any weight given to mentoring by the profession and there needs to be accreditation before this is changed', whilst at the other extreme a mentor 'sought to undertake the work because I believed that it was something for the future and as second in department I needed to have something to offer, besides it taught me a lot about my teaching'. From the responses it seems that the career progression is seen to be of greater importance to those mentors who were not yet head of department because of its value in seeking promotion.

Policies and consequences

Control and monitoring

Three patterns of control and monitoring are evident in the case study schools. In two schools there is a strong hierarchical management with the head believing that he is to carry out the contractual arrangement with the college and that 'as an agent the school has to meet these needs fully'. In a further nine schools the head and senior management team determine the policy within which the scheme will operate and then delegate operation to the professional mentor. The problems of this are summed up in one response as

> once the policy has been delegated to the professional mentor there is no further senior management involvement and he maintains all the links with the college ... as a result the subject staff call the tune and the student may not always be getting what the SMT think they have set up.

In the remaining nine schools the control is even more tenuous as the professional mentor is left with total responsibility for policy and organisation. However, in three of these schools there is evidence of a degree of collegial planning where 'the mentor team agrees policy with the professional mentor to secure uniformity of practice'. Within this succession the role of the HEI appears to diminish as schools develop their own interpretation of contractual arrangements.

Perceptions of the degree of HEI control and monitoring vary according to the distance of the professional mentor from the line management contact to the HEI. The system is seen to be less constraining where the professional mentor carries the responsibility but where the head or deputy is responsible, there is a greater willingness to go directly to the HEI in the event of problems. The HEI tutors, with much reduced time allocations and with a view that the responsibility is now with the professional mentors, are unwilling to be too readily available.

The issues which present problems in monitoring and control are mainly associated with 'the way in which associates have been prepared for their work in their subject', 'the assessment of work which is set by staff who do not see how the school or the subject is organised', 'the provision of support for weaker associates where the amount of time taken can cause severe problems for a department or a professional mentor', 'the inadequacy of funding for the work which it is expected that the schools will do, especially during the first and third terms when the associates are on less readily supervised programmes', and 'the need for some form of quality assurance from the HEI because they are leaving us to set our own standards and we do need to know that their tutors are doing something to ensure consistency'. Above all the main concern is with 'the determination of the pass-fail borderline for the main practice – it hasn't been a problem yet but we are all worried that there will come a time when we are on our own and when the college will not be able to help because they will not be fully in the picture despite the procedures which they have set up'.

Partnership

The list of issues outlined above is symptomatic of the establishment of relationships within the partnership 'which is often spoken about but which doesn't really exist in practice'. The evidence suggests that where the guidelines for mentoring have been developed by a joint group of school and HEI staff there is a more favourable perception of the arrangements. Of the questionnaire respondents, all from mentors within one partnership, 92% see the present partnership arrangements as a positive move with 63% believing that the present balance is most effective in matching 'control with opportunity in the real world'. In the fourteen schools from all three partnerships which have been part of the planning and organisational process the current problems arise from administrative rather than structural problems or are connected with 'needing further guidelines for the support and assessment of weaker students' or 'the need for a better set of arrangements for the summer weeks', or 'for some system which allows us to know who is coming and to make arrangements well in advance'. For most of these schools the partnership is evolving and there are mechanisms for the representation of ideas of schools to HEI and vice versa. In the remaining six schools, which for some reason were not part of the original planning procedure, the arrangements were presented by the HEI and there has been a long period of adjustment with difficulties arising from the student profile assessment system, a fundamental misunderstanding by schools of the contractual input of subject tutors, and a misunderstanding of pedagogic requirements.

There have been certain barriers to the successful evolution of a partnership. These have included 'the view in some schools that they are acting as our agents and not as an equal in the training process', ' a feeling that the underfunding is so bad that the school does not want to be involved', 'a view that the school is neglected by the HEI especially in coping with marginal students', and 'no clear understanding of why the HEI gets over £4,000 but we only get £800 for our work'. The development of professional and subject mentor meetings has been beneficial and well received where the partnership is strengthened through demanding and consultative meetings 'rather than a lightweight session on how to cope with profile reports'.

At the same time schools seek to maintain their own interpretation of partnership guidelines and practices. Three of the schools make clear their view 'that college guidelines have to be interpreted in the light of school needs but the scheme is workable', 'that the evolution of a quality course is based on the interpretation and understanding of guidelines reinforced by professionalism', and 'the role of the HEI might be strengthened if it were to become a moderator so that we were sure that we were demanding the right standards'.

There is a general view that the support given by the HEI is appropriate given the contractual arrangements. Communications between partner elements are seen to be well managed by 68% of the respondents, with 63% believing that there is a commonality of view between HEI and school staff and 82% perceiving support for the mentors by the HEI.

Financial management

The allocation of resources has already been considered in its impact on the schools. There is evidence that policy practice varies between HEIs and schools and within schools. The range of experience is between the heavily centralised where 'the money is allocated by the university and we have to accept that we cannot change it', to the individualised where the 'allocation of the money is as a lump to the mentoring team who are then responsible for the allocation within school'. The deficiencies of the system are thus related to the HEI in some schools, and yet in others this is taken as a starting point for collegial allocation. Half of the schools have payments 'made within an atmosphere of secrecy'. The situation is much more open in a further six schools where 'the information is published by the SMT but is generally not of interest except to the mentoring team'. It may be that the additional responsibility is so much of a bolt on activity that it is not regarded as general school policy. The liability to micropolitical tensions is a reflection of this.

Value for money

The case study reports do give an indication of the value for money consequent upon a shift of responsibilities. Both the direct and indirect costs have been evaluated on a continuum from positive, or beneficial, to negative, or inhibiting the real work of the school. Direct costs are seen to be at their highest 'where the support of a weak associate might well take a department over the top', a sentiment expressed by three schools, and where 'the impact on staff time is out of proportion to the benefits resulting from the presence of the associate', as noted in ten of the schools. There is particular mention of the problems which might arise in the earlier stages of classroom management. One school noted the 'disruption to normal class teacher contact', and another the 'time taken with the preparation of the associate so that he or she is sufficiently aware of the subject content to be left to get on with the teaching'.

The indirect costs to the staff and school as a whole are seen to arise in five schools from the time taken by administrative, ancillary and departmental staff to 'support the associates, especially when there is a knock on effect of the need to give them a lot of support in the early stages', 'the need for some support to replace the immediate back up which the HEI used to give', and 'the time taken by the staff to support students outside the classroom situation'. Two schools comment on the underfunding and the pressures which having the associates places upon the resource structure of the school. The extent of this worry may be seen in that one school feels 'that the returns are inadequate overall to induce further participation', and another comments that 'the costs are too great and if the pressures continue we shall reach breaking point'.

Schools have, however, realised the benefits accruing from associate participation. Within the classroom 'there is an increased opportunity for flexible teaching arrangements, the development of new approaches and the making of additional materials' and staff comment in two schools on 'the way in which the associates can give a new dimension to some subject developments'. Other advantages may be summed up in 'the countless little ways of staff support', 'the pay back in the third term', and 'the availability of an extra pair of hands within the department'. Three schools detail consideration of new teaching approaches, three report on the opportunity to do things differently, and four comment on 'the improved ratio for some teaching activities'.

The balance of advantage from involvement is summed up in the report on one school which comments that

> ITT was teacher training on the cheap, and it was suggested that the HEI was not sufficiently sensitive to the demands being made upon the school in general and the mentors in particular. The partnership schools had to feel that there was value for money or else they would withdraw from the arrangement sooner rather than later.

Interaction and impact

We return now to our earlier assertion that the quality of the experience of the associate was affected by the strength of resource and pedagogic support and the attitude of mentor, department and school to the changed arrangements for initial teacher training. The recruitment, training and retention of mentors appears to play a major part in determining the effectiveness of the training for individual students. Once appointed mentors are offered training of varying content and quality. This may have an emphasis on developmental support for students , or it may be more concerned with the procedures necessary to ensure that there is consistency in the treatment of all students on a course. Variation may then occur because of the responses of mentors dependent upon their attitude to the work or their structural position in the school. Support, assessment and development require additional time input and at its extreme may involve up to three additional hours per day where an associate is developing competencies in a subject such as science, or where the associate has problems which require constant attention. Not surprisingly, and compounded by the personal and professional pressures which a mentor may be experiencing, commitment, motivation and attitude to the associate may be variously affected.

The associate will usually be working in a subject area in which several other teaching and non-teaching staff are involved. The other staff will be involved in providing training opportunities or simply by supporting the work undertaken within the department. Where the mentoring agreement is for the associate to work with the classes of the mentor alone, the departmental responsibility is minimised although other colleagues may have an influence and offer a listening ear. It is not only in its general atmosphere but in the overall attitude to the provision of resources and the opening up of training experiences that a department can affect associates' development. Our evidence further suggests that the organisational context of the mentoring activity may also have supportive or inhibiting influence on associate satisfaction since the status of mentoring will affect the final outcomes.

The atmosphere for training engendered by the school as a community may be influenced by a range of variables. This will include the attitudes of the senior management team, however designated, the shared values of the staff, the level of professional competence of the mentors and the availability of resources. Where associates are seen as a necessary evil, managed, but not developed, by a professional mentor who is a member of a hard-pressed senior team without either time or recognition for the liaison work necessary, the attitude of the school staff as a whole tends to see the activity as an additional burden, often with limited empathy or support for the training process. Where the associates are accepted as part of a whole school policy, and where this work is integrated with the general professional development of staff, our evidence is of positive and productive relationships. In three of the twenty schools studied the 'bolt-on' nature of teacher training was detrimental to the experience of associates. It is our contention that there is a more positive environment where all staff are working towards standards of classroom management and mutual respect. This enables the associate to be more rapidly assimilated into the school and mentoring to be successful.

These three determinants of the mentoring environment can act in ways which are supportive of the associate or they can be unhelpful, and negative in a way which the associate considers to be counter-productive. In a minority of placements, there may be personality mismatches on the part of either associate or mentor which intensify the structural effects of the mentoring environment.

Our evidence, drawn from interview responses, indicates that there are recognisable broadly based descriptors for each element in the total training environment. These provide a framework for understanding and analysis of the training process. The two extremes are the supportive, marked by positive attitudes, planned experiences and an integrated approach to the initial teacher training responsibilities, and the adverse where the attitudes suggest that the associates are either a nuisance or another pair of hands, where the experiences are random and the atmosphere one of cynicism and mistrust.

Discussion with associates also indicates that the three elements may be ranked with a declining impact upon associate development though this, of course, varies with each individual experience. Those closest to the associate have the most influence on the mentoring environment especially where the experience is of short duration, or where the placement is in a large institution such as a tertiary college. Interview evidence suggests that the influence of the school culture is actually quite strong 'because it makes a difference to the attitudes of the staff room and if that is generally warm and welcoming then everything else seems to go right' (associate comment). Normally the ranking of influence declines from that of the mentor, to the other members of the department, and thence to the school, but this may be disturbed because of personalities, local circumstances and the particular organisational issues such as redundancy which might cloud the readiness to receive and support associates.

The influence of mentors may be tempered by the other responsibilities they carry, by their age and length of time in teaching, by their attitude to change and by their professional commitment and aspirations. The department may be a micropolitical arena into which the associate has been unwittingly launched. Their impact on the associate is greatest if he or she works with more than one member of staff, and if attitudes reflect a commonality of purpose and a team spirit or the antithesis of this in a group which suspects the motivation, and is overtly critical of the practices, of colleagues. The influence of the school is yet more complex and appears to be related to the age and social structure of the staff, the folklore of past student experience, shared loyalty, and the degree of willingness to open up activities and discussions to comparative strangers. In short, the complexity of influences is considerable and we recognise that the collection of a number of characteristics within the three elements given whilst relatively simplistic at this stage, nevertheless gives a basis for considering an analytical model. (Glover *et al.*, 1994).

The value of the work to date has been that it has yielded a set of descriptors which enable the training situation to be categorised and we have been able to analyse the relationships and potential for success within each of the case study schools and colleges.

The most successful training environment appears to be one where the senior staff of the school has developed a policy for associate training as part of a total staff development policy, negotiated the payment in time and money as part of a total package for involvement, and where the concept of the training school has become part of the culture. Within this school the departments are being progressively trained in mentoring skills, the team teaching culture is strong and the assessment process for associates mirrors the appraisal activity within the team. The mentors are then fully trained, and all are pursuing accreditation for the work and the development of a resource base to foster the activity. They prize the weekly time allocation for the work which they are undertaking.

The schools concerned are aware of the need to set the initial teacher training work within the policy framework of the school. Three schools mention the need for self-evaluative techniques for 'the mentors and the associates to review each others' work', 'the inculcation of a reflective mode of thinking about subject and staff development' and 'to evaluate departments within the school context'. Five schools point to the need for a joint evaluation from the HEI but only two of the schools see 'new opportunities for research in the partnership between school and the university world'. This indicates that the research potential of the partnership has not yet been exploited

The evidence of changing attitudes is strong. In the case study investigations the staff concerned were asked to outline future plans. As the scheme of association develops the schools appear to be more prepared to look at it in semi-permanent terms. Three of the twenty schools make suggestions that the demands on time and personnel may be such that they will not be long term members of the scheme but fourteen of the case studies show that the schools are prepared to develop the partnership through a variety of policy changes including 'the development of best practice from successful mentoring departments to other areas of the school', 'the encouragement of a mentoring culture in other aspects of professional development', 'the full involvement of associates in the staffroom and with parents so that they are seen as part of the school', and 'the development of opportunities for the link tutor to be used within the school so that the partnership has an identifiable focus'.

The reports suggest that the partnership is strengthening through joint training, 'major changes in the attitude of staff to each other and to the associates, as a newer understanding of roles becomes known', 'improved accreditation opportunities' and 'the integration of all aspects of professional development work in association with the HEI'. There are however, strong cautionary words in six study reports. In essence these urge that 'the current balance of time between HEI and schools has to work because the schools cannot do more'. The policy implications of this are that some schools see their future as training schools whilst others feel that they would be better not associated with such schemes – in those the mentoring culture may well be adverse at the present time.

CHAPTER 6

Working with Beginning Teachers: the impact on schools

Stephen Carney and Hazel Hagger

Introduction

The Oxford Internship Scheme, a school-based PGCE Secondary course, was launched in 1987 following two years of planning involving the University of Oxford Department of Educational Studies, Oxfordshire Local Education Authority and Oxfordshire secondary schools. The course sought to give much more significance to the distinctive expertise of practising teachers, and also to operationalise a new conception of the relation between theory and practice in the education of student teachers.

In order to make sense of what follows, it is necessary briefly to describe some aspects of the scheme. The student teachers – called *interns* – are attached to a single school for most of the PGCE year. From October to mid-January they spend two days per week in the school and the remainder of the time in the university. This period is known as *J-* or *Joint weeks*. From January until the end of May – *S-* or *School weeks* – they spend virtually all their time in school. At the conclusion of S-weeks interns spend a further three weeks in another school gaining an Alternative Experience (*AE weeks*). In each school there are typically eight to ten interns, usually in subject pairs. In school, the two key staff roles in relation to the scheme are:

- *mentors:* subject specialists who each guide and co-ordinate two interns' school-based learning in relation to classroom teaching;
- *professional tutors:* usually senior teachers who each co-ordinate their own school's work in initial teacher education and take direct responsibility for the school-based learning of the group of interns in relation to whole-school issues (the Professional Development Programme).

By 1994, when the Esmée Fairbairn project commenced, the partnership between Oxfordshire schools and the University was firmly established. In the first instance, therefore, partner schools were invited to discuss with the researchers issues of interest or concern in relation to school-based initial teacher education and to outline possible areas for investigation. In this way, schools were able both to articulate their particular concerns and play a central role in designing the research strategies; the role of the university partners was to shape these expressed concerns into workable research proposals.

Within the framework outlined above, five investigations were carried out in four secondary schools in Oxfordshire. Two of the investigations are discussed together as both were concerned with the relationship between provision for student teachers and for Newly Qualified Teachers. The discussion that follows is arranged under four headings:

- ITE and the role of non-mentors
- student teachers and newly qualified staff
- student teachers and the impact on students
- ITE and the benefits for teachers

ITE and the role of non-mentors

The teachers who had instigated this investigation felt that arrangements in school departments were not always sufficient to ensure that subject teachers other than mentors were able to contribute fully as members of the teacher education team. In particular, they sought to understand the ways in which subject teachers worked with interns and related to mentors, and to clarify the support that they received.

Data was collected in two stages. Firstly, interviews were conducted both with selected staff and with others randomly selected from across the school. There was a particular focus on one department where it was hoped that a detailed picture of the working arrangements in relation to internship would emerge.

Secondly, these findings – in the form of an Interim Report – were presented to staff for consideration and their reflections formed the basis for a series of final comments. The issues emerging from the first round of data collection are now discussed in turn.

Subject teachers' engagement in internship

Firstly, it was clear that subject teachers worked with interns in many different ways. The extent of classroom support and guidance varied and subject teachers described many different approaches. A common one was for the interns themselves to establish the type and amount of support they needed. One subject teacher explained:

Usually when they first start, I like to leave them alone if they want it because you can imagine that they are very nervous. They [current interns] have wanted my involvement at the beginning. And also they have wanted – particularly Jenny – a lesson each week, at least, checked, observed in one way or another. In that sense, the involvement has been great but it has really been the interns who have told me what they're having to look at each week.

Subject teachers cited a range of strategies for 'giving over' classes to interns as they progressed through their school experience. Some involved themselves in formal planning, observation and de-briefing with interns throughout the school experience whilst others gave interns independence at an early stage.

Subject teachers' dealings with mentors were overwhelmingly described as informal. Mentors gave general advice on internship and on the progress of individual interns but subject teachers considered it to be their own responsibility to plan and manage activities related to the work of interns with their own classes. At least three subject teachers suggested that there was little talk (or need for talk) between themselves and mentors because of the quality of the particular intern. One mentor thought that 'good self-evaluative interns' were able to 'prompt' colleagues and often, the amount of discussion between subject teachers and the mentor was determined by the perceived competence of the intern.

Learning to work with interns

When asked how they learnt to work with interns, subject teachers talked of such things as 'instinct', 'maturity' and 'experience' – factors related more to their individual professional expertise and experience in the classroom than to any formal training or preparation. Mentors often supported this when explaining their criteria for selecting subject teachers:

I think I make big, sweeping assumptions really, just based on personality and how open they are going to be and what you know of their teaching style.

Subject teachers did, however, claim to receive various kinds of help, including prompt sheets of learning objectives, feedback from the mentor on interns' progress and observing the university curriculum tutor undertaking de-briefings with interns.

Subject teachers and the management of interns' learning

In terms of how subject teachers worked with mentors there appeared once again to be great differences between departments. Some subject teachers were happy with the degree of freedom afforded them by mentors whilst others were unhappy that they were largely ignorant of the interns' overall progress and learning needs. In some departments internship was discussed regularly with all involved staff: mentors provided guidance on what subject teachers should be focusing on with interns and also updated them on the interns' general progress. In these cases subject teachers claimed that their views and opinions were taken into account and used to promote the interns' learning across the department. One subject teacher explained:

> I think she [the mentor] needs to know as much about their progress as possible because she can't get a broad picture just from the lessons they take of hers.

It must be noted however that not all subject teachers desired regular and detailed information relating to the progress and work of interns. Some were happy with occasional notification and involvement, acknowledging it was not their responsibility to be considering the overall progress of interns. Indicating some difference of perception, mentors claimed to provide a great deal of information to subject teachers in terms of interns' needs and to offer considerable guidance for assessing their progress. In all departments informal approaches (talking 'around the kettle' between lessons) seemed to be more prevalent than formal meetings between mentors and subject teachers.

Importantly, whilst mentors conceded that there was scope for colleagues to play a more central role in the interns' experience in the department they themselves were reluctant to impose any such role:

> Because teachers don't like to be taught by other people – some of them at least – and that's where I don't want to be. I want to be helping and saying 'Yes, this is great' or 'Uhmm, have you noticed that …' and 'I think this is a really interesting way of doing it, isn't it?' rather than 'This is a really good approach that I think you ought to try'.

Constraints for subject teachers

Many subject teachers said that they had insufficient time to devote to their work with interns and that they often had difficulty in finding the time for discussion with the mentor. Furthermore, many subject teachers suggested that their role in internship was unclear. This lack of clarity was perceived by the interns who frequently referred to the subject teacher/ mentor relationship as 'confused'.

> I'm not sure whether non-mentor teachers were aware of their role in, say, evaluating a lesson. The feedback I get at the end of a … lesson would be subject-based more than an overall learning and teaching technique. If I had done it with [the mentor] she would have spent more time on that.

Mentors, however, thought that subject teachers, far from being marginal figures, were key members of the department's initial teacher education team but that this was rarely spelled out.

Improving the work of subject teachers in internship

During the initial phase of interviewing, teachers and interns were asked to describe what could ideally be provided in order to improve the work of subject teachers in internship. They suggested the following possibilities:

- greater access to the mentor in order to understand more fully the learning needs and priorities of interns
- more opportunities as a department to discuss teacher education commitments formally
- written guidelines for subject teachers working with student teachers

Whilst many subject teachers felt that they would benefit from a greater involvement with the mentor, few were prepared to advocate formal meetings which implied further demands on their time. Some saw the department meeting, for a number of reasons, as an ideal forum and suggested that internship should be a regular agenda item where colleagues were able to 'feed into mentors' understanding' and where internship could 'inform and promote school practices'. In this way some thought that internship might help to create opportunities for discussion among colleagues. Others, however, thought the department meeting lacked the focus to discuss internship and was an 'awkward' forum because of the presence of the interns themselves; most thought that interns should be present at department meetings as this was an important sign that they were being treated as full members of the department.

Most subject teachers felt that written guidelines produced specifically for their use would be helpful in facilitating work with interns. One subject teacher wanted to see a 'mini mentor handbook ...with bullet points' which could be 'something where you could skim though' to get a quick understanding of the interns' learning programme and their needs. The notion of a written resource specifically for subject teachers was strongly endorsed by mentors. In stressing the need for such guidelines to be produced by the university partner, mentors underlined the difficulties they faced when attempting to carry out their responsibilities as managers of interns' learning in their department:

> If they have a mini-booklet that's actually produced by the university I suppose it's got a bit more status than me just photocopying a sheet and saying 'Here you are'.

The reluctance of mentors to encourage and guide subject teachers' work with interns suggested that much of the potential impact of this work with interns was being lost:

> Because the mentor never goes far enough in sharing their own understanding and skills it jars – it doesn't really work well. So you limit it. You don't want

to be too pushy, you don't want to take up too much of their time and therefore the whole experience is being limited in terms of what it could provide.

Mentors argued that by recognising and promoting subject teachers as teacher educators, the status of subject teachers within the school could be enhanced. This, it was thought, was essential if subject teachers were to give their work with interns appropriate attention and if mentors were to see their departmental colleagues as crucial to the quality of student teacher learning outcomes.

Preliminary recommendations

Drawing on the suggestions of mentors and other subject teachers, and also more generally on the interview findings, the second and final stage of this investigation sought reactions from school staff in different positions to the Interim Report which contained a number of possible ways forward. These included:

- persuading subject teachers that they are significant members of the school's initial teacher education team, responsible for the interns' professional training and development. This message needed to come not only from the mentor and school professional tutor but also from heads of departments and the headteacher. The headteacher could indicate the importance of this commitment by allocating school INSET time to internship where the skills and strategies involved in working with novices could be examined.
- obtaining consensus within the department about the precise roles of non-mentor subject teachers by devoting a departmental meeting to clarifying these arrangements. Here, the mentor and the university curriculum tutor could explain the aims and principles of internship, make suggestions and respond to concerns expressed by other members of the department. The head of department should take the lead in establishing this consensus.
- ensuring that effective and regular liaison between the mentor and subject colleagues by devoting a part of every department meeting to a discussion of the progress and needs of individual interns
- ensuring that non-mentor subject teachers receive appropriate guidance on how to work individually with interns by the production of brief and straightforward written guidelines

Reactions to the recommendations

Responses to the Interim Report were recorded by interview (in the case of the headteacher and the professional tutor) and by a questionnaire to all staff recently or currently engaged in internship. In general, staff supported the recommendations. The headteacher and heads of departments were both seen as essential for the establishment of a commitment to teacher education across the school. All respondents saw subject teachers as essential members of department ITE teams and as such INSET and the production of written guidelines to support their contribution were viewed favourably.

Commentary

One of the most difficult aspects of the mentor's role is that of managing student teachers' learning across a whole subject department and its classes. Many other teachers seem quite keen to be involved, but the terms on which they can most fruitfully and realistically be involved are not obvious. This study has highlighted issues – such as time, general understanding of the ITE scheme, ongoing communication, a need for autonomy and a need to be consulted, and a clear sense of having ITE as a recognised part of their job – as possible conditions for their effective involvement. Resolution of problems would seem to depend on universities taking an active role in confronting the issue and developing agreed guidelines within their partnerships; on strong leadership and clear thinking from both head teachers and heads of department; and perhaps on the mentor role having a less ambivalent status.

Student teachers and newly qualified staff

Two schools were interested in the arrangements in place for student teachers (predominantly interns) and newly qualified staff. Both had an established provision for these groups and to this extent the investigations shared much in common.

One of the schools (School X) was concerned with understanding how, as a relatively small institution, it could accommodate large numbers of student teachers (interns and others) and of NQTs. How could it do so satisfactorily without asking experienced teachers to neglect their primary task of teaching pupils? Was there any scope for rationalisation of its provision for the two groups? Was there any scope for useful collaboration between members of the two groups?

School Y was interested in learning more about the way in which its provision for student teachers and NQTs worked in practice, and was perceived by staff in general. At this school it was hoped that an investigation might ascertain the elements of an ideal provision for both groups as well as consider ways in which these groups could usefully work more closely together to develop their classroom teaching.

Both investigations involved extended interviews with interns and their mentors, with NQTs and their assigned teachers, with professional tutors, and with other subject teachers. At School X interviews were conducted once in the Spring term and sought the perspectives of a range of staff, particularly those in three nominated departments. The interviews focused on the nature of the provision for both groups, the distinctive practices of the departments and the possibilities for collaborative classroom arrangements. The investigation in School Y attempted to consider the school's provision for both groups over an entire academic year and interviews were conducted with relevant staff in each of the three terms. In both schools interns and newly qualified staff were interviewed extensively.

Interns

In both schools the relationship between interns and mentors followed very much the guidelines established by the Internship Partnership. There was timetabled support for interns from assigned subject mentors who were responsible for co-ordinating their learning across the department. Interns also participated in a co-ordinated set of weekly whole–school sessions and received general and classroom support from university curriculum tutors throughout the year. As they moved through the year and took on increased responsibilities in and for lessons they received support from the mentor, other subject teachers, the professional tutor and university tutors. This process culminated in the interns taking responsibility for classes and for evaluating their own progress.

This quite highly structured and comprehensive provision appeared to be generally satisfactory to the various groups involved. Among the concerns expressed, three were especially relevant to this investigation.

Factors underlying variation in provision for interns

While interns in both schools praised the work and enthusiasm of their mentors, it was apparent that the quality of support that they were given varied across departments. Among the factors underlying this variation, one seemed to be the extent of mentors' 'other commitments'.

Another was the readiness of mentors to accept responsibility as managers of the interns' learning, with some claiming that it was the responsibility of interns to 'ask for help' if it was needed.

Difficulties for professional tutors in leading ITE teams

The professional tutor in School X was highly conscientious, had protected time for this role, and was much appreciated by interns for her availability and supportiveness. She was especially aware, however, of the problems involved in leading mentor colleagues with regard to the ways in which they worked with interns in their departments:

It's very difficult to have a policy, as it were. I find it very difficult not to be too interfering. I don't think it's my role to interfere too much to make sure that every single intern is having the same quality of mentoring, It's difficult to standardise.

The marginality of work other than subject teaching

Interns' overwhelming priorities throughout the year were focused on their subject teaching work in classrooms. Anything else, such as their weekly whole-school seminars with professional tutors, was much less important and, as with occasional university-based days in S-weeks, might well be seen as a disruption of this important work. In so far as they saw themselves as learners, the important learning was in the context of their school subject departments.

Consensus about internship provision

A questionnaire drawing on previous internship publications (Hagger *et al.*, 1993; Rothwell *et al.*, 1994) and outlining a possible ideal provision for student teachers was presented to all staff in School Y.

Of the twenty elements suggested, the following 12 were considered to be 'essential' by a majority of the teachers. It would appear then that generally speaking staff endorsed the practices in relation to working with student teachers that had been established within internship:

- full induction into the practices and procedures of the department
- a designated mentor who has been fully inducted into the internship scheme
- mentor's support and guidance for lesson planning to help interns develop competence in planning skills
- protected timetabled time with the mentor (possibly more than one lesson per week)
- recognition by the school that subject teachers' work with interns is important and time consuming if undertaken properly
- time for subject teachers to engage in observation and de-briefing of interns
- gradual and structured introduction into work in classes
- opportunities to work with and observe departmental colleagues throughout the year in order to experience a range of different teaching strategies
- account taken of interns' distinctive needs and concerns which reflect the progression of their own learning
- opportunities to observe and work with groups of different ages and abilities throughout the year but especially in S-weeks
- approximately 50–60% of a full timetable by the S-weeks phase in

which interns can take a significant responsibility for the work of classes

- support of subject teachers who are enthusiastic, informed about the aims and processes of internship and briefed by mentors on the overall progress and needs of the interns

Newly qualified teachers

The overall provision for NQTs varied somewhat between the two schools. In School X it was irregular, largely unstructured and fragmented, with provision seen as the concern of subject departments. The deputy head with responsibility for NQTs explained:

> In structured departments, the training they receive there is far better than anything I can give them because it's classroom-based...Departments are given certain autonomy and therefore heads of departments, very properly, monitor progress of the NQTs within their own training programmes.

Whilst the deputy head claimed that there were a number of centrally provided elements to the provision, it was clear that NQTs were expected to gain greatest benefits from their work in the classroom. To this end they were given a teaching load 'slightly less than someone in their second year of teaching' and were exposed to the full range of classes, but were generally protected from providing cover for other staff.

Most provision for NQTs was reactive. They were expected to play a role in assessing their own needs and to specify appropriate support from the deputy head and others. Subject teachers, including heads of departments suggested that their role in the NQTs' development was unclear.

Some teachers expressed the view that the first priority of newly qualified staff was to establish themselves in their classes and departments. In this regard the deputy head suggested that the school had the same expectations of NQTs as it had of any other teacher and that they 'just need to get on with it'. However, this was not to say that NQTs were neglected within the school. In fact the main elements of the provision supported the proposition that rather than being learners, NQTs were fully competent professionals who needed time and space to consolidate and develop their practice.

In School Y the provision for NQTs was extensive and well supported. Each NQT was allocated an assigned teacher who had time-tabled time in which to fulfil the role. There were also regular half-term review meetings with heads of department and the professional tutor which were informed by lesson observations. NQTs had access to INSET and were encouraged to attend a minimum number of central NQT sessions co-ordinated by the professional tutor. Both NQTs and their assigned teachers regarded the extent of this provision as a substantial commitment on the part of this school to preparing NQTs for their teaching career. The elements of this provision with a number of additional ideal components was documented and presented to staff. Interestingly, there was much less agreement about the suggested provision than was the case for the provision for interns and only the following elements were considered essential by the majority of school staff:

- a comprehensive induction to the school both in the July preceding their appointment and in the week prior to the commencement of the Autumn term
- an assigned teacher fully inducted into the role of guiding NQTs
- comprehensive and well organised schemes of work materials and other teaching resources

The relative lack of agreement on the provision for NQTs suggests at least two things. Firstly, as in School X, there was a concern to ensure NQTs were properly inducted into the procedures and the ways of working within the school. Secondly, both NQTs and experienced staff seemed sceptical about any structured provision for NQTs which either distracted them from their classroom teaching or implied that they were not fully competent to undertake that teaching. NQTs were certainly keen to meet with other NQTs and key staff. But the existing provision in this school generally did not relate closely enough to NQTs' classroom teaching, and suggested that provision related to classroom teaching seemed to be viewed as undermining NQTs' status.

Possibilities for collaboration between interns and NQTs

In both schools there was a general concern that interns and NQTs were not interacting as much as was possible and that benefits from such interaction existed for both groups. Staff were therefore prepared to suggest a number of possible collaborative arrangements:

- occasional shared sessions on topics of mutual interest such as school/ parent relationships, role of governors, national curriculum and assessment
- mutual support, talking and sharing of ideas and experiences in departments
- joint planning and observation activities
- collaborative teaching

Staff in both schools had reservations about intern/NQT collaboration in the classroom and tended to assume that any such collaboration would place NQTs in an evaluation and assessment role. A number, however, mentioned useful possibilities both in and out of the classroom:

We've done team teaching with the interns which has helped...We've sat and planned lessons together and divided it up into how we're going to teach it and that's been very helpful. We are sharing ideas and they are being given ideas by someone with a bit more experience than them. (NQT)

I think it would be quite advantageous if NQTs and interns had some joint sessions ... where you sit down and have a specific problem or topic to discuss. It's quite valuable for the interns to see that yes, you can progress. (subject teacher)

It might actually be quite nice for them [the interns] to see that you have survived – you're still alive! (NQT)

Actually it's quite good for the NQTs. From my own point of view I like to continually monitor my own teaching...and when you hear the interns talking about that if you've not been used to that system, it's a very good opportunity. So there's a lot of cross referencing that can be done which I think in joint sessions can be raised. (subject teacher)

Many staff also suggested that provision for both interns and NQTs could be enhanced if overall responsibility for their development were invested in one person.

Commentary

What relationship should there be, if any, between schools' provision for NQTs and for student teachers ? It is surely significant that two schools independently raised this as a matter for investigation. Yet in the same two schools the general consensus among staff seemed to be that NQTs and student teachers need to be understood in quite different ways. It is true that both thrive only in their classroom habitat. But student teachers are learners, and need support for their learning; NQTs on the other hand, are teachers and need to be left to get on with it. Of course, student teachers do a lot of teaching, and of course NQTs have a lot to learn. But NQTs feel that what they most need is recognition as proper teachers, and other teachers tend to support this. In contrast, there seems to be general acceptance that what student teachers most need is to learn.

At least for the present, it is within the framework of this firm distinction that schools have to consider the possibilities and problems in relation to student teachers and NQTs. There seems no easy way of escaping the common-sense truth that if the ratio of NQTs *and* student teachers to experienced teachers is very high, there will be pressure on every one and, other things being equal, every one will be less well served. However, creative thinking about provision for professional development, including possible relationships between that for NQTs and that for student teachers, is severely constrained where there is not an integrated and prestigious management structure for professional learning and development within which heads of department are heavily involved.

Student teachers and the impact on pupils

A third investigation focused on the whole-school implications of internship and specifically, the year on year effects for a school of hosting large numbers of interns. In particular the school wished to learn more about the ways in which mentors and other staff working with interns took account of the pupils' learning needs; how staff monitored the learning of pupils who were working with interns; how pupils viewed interns' teaching; and whether pupils differentiated between their normal class teacher and the interns in relation to perceived learning outcomes.

Mentors in two subject departments were interviewed to discuss their plans for interns' classroom teaching and generally to describe the ways in which they and their colleagues worked with the interns in the department. Interns were observed teaching two classes in different years before being interviewed to discuss the lesson, how it related to their plans, how they had been working with the class and more generally the arrangements in the department that had helped their learning and work with pupils. A number of pupils in each of these classes were interviewed after each observed lesson and asked about their opinion of the subject, the nature of their work with the intern, the perceived differences to that with their normal teacher and the impact on their learning, if any, of having interns in their classes. This process occurred twice, over the Spring and Summer terms.

From the data two broad themes emerged. Firstly, both pupils and mentors claimed positive benefits from the work of interns with their classes. Secondly, the extent of these benefits, particularly to pupils, depended crucially on the arrangements in place in departments to support the work and learning of interns with classes. It is now useful to expand upon each of these themes.

Pupils' perceptions of interns' teaching

When pupils were asked to consider the differences between the lessons taught by the intern and those delivered by their usual teacher, a range of perceptions were offered. All pupils in one subject thought that their classes with the intern were either 'more fun' or 'less serious'. Typical comments included:

> I think [the intern] makes the lessons more fun, we learn more because we're paying attention.

> It's nice with her, she's thoughtful when she's teaching us. She sort of makes it fun. She likes talking to us rather than just teaching and that's it.

Pupils explained these perceptions in different ways. Many suggested that the interns, as younger teachers, were able to relate more closely to them:

> I think they both try and make lessons fun, but I think because [the intern], I think she's younger than [the teacher], it makes it a bit better.

> Well, I think I probably feel more comfortable talking to [the intern] than [the teacher], probably because she's younger. We don't always stick to the lesson, we talk about other things.

In terms of classroom interactions, many students across both subjects and across both years felt that the interns offered more individual attention, were better listeners and tried to develop better relationships. One felt that interns were more likely to move around the classroom, ask questions and assist students whereas the normal teacher was more inclined to be seen as unapproachable and 'usually sitting at the desk marking things'. Another student saw the intern as 'more of a friend than a teacher' and yet another thought that the intern made more of an effort to get on with students.

Many students suggested that this had implications for their work. In one subject a number of students felt that in the intern's class they were inclined to contribute more. Another two suggested that they 'work better' and another offered 'I ask for more help'. Others suggested 'I've got more personality in my work' and 'I'm more confident and put my hand up and things'. In the other subject observed, students across both years felt that interns used the board and OHP more, provided more worksheets, more experiments and were inclined to 'show more'. In some cases Year 7 students felt that the intern's worksheets were more demanding.

With regard to the question of perceived differences between the intern and their normal teacher, pupils' responses were generally consistent in both phases of data collection. Almost half of those interviewed in one subject and the majority in another suggested that they were unable to 'rank' one teacher above the other. Descriptions of both of them as 'thoughtful',' interesting' and 'making lessons fun' were commonplace. Importantly, no student felt that the interns were harming their learning.

A few pupils, however, suggested that the superior subject knowledge of the normal class teacher and her greater experience meant that their preparation for examinations would be better than it would with the intern. Another noted that their joint class (conducted by two interns with the mentor in a supporting role) had particular benefits:

> Even if [intern no. 1] is talking to us, if he's missed something then [intern no. 2] will always kind of like chip in. They do that quite often, which helps. Because with three teachers you get more.

It was clear that many of the younger students did not regard the interns as trainee teachers. In one class students appeared genuinely surprised when the intern announced that she was returning to the university to complete her course; one even wanted to know if the school had sacked her!

Year 7 students in particular were more likely to view the interns as normal, although less experienced, teachers who were working closely with the more established staff:

> I think they [intern and teacher] make a good team actually.

> I think they're learning off each other about new things and stuff.

Mentors' perceptions of the overall impact of interns on the work of their departments

Mentors claimed that interns had a positive impact on pupil learning in many different ways. These included:

- increased attention to and resources for individual pupils
- new insights into the nature and needs of individual pupils
- enhanced communication within departments

Both mentors pointed out that interns supported their work with classes and enabled them to achieve much more, especially in relation to student learning. As a consequence of the partnership with the intern they felt able to spend more time with individual pupils, to assess and discuss work more quickly, to gain new understandings of their pupils and to engage in discussions about their progress and needs.

Additionally, mentors found their involvement with interns to be of personal benefit as well as a catalyst for improved communication in the department:

> Because we have to be explicit about what we're doing, therefore we have to articulate our aims ... And when you're working with an intern you can't just wander into the classroom and make the lesson up. You have to talk to them about what you're going to do and I think that's good for you as well.

> I like the other interns as well being in the staff room. It just means that the school can't get away with just working its own little code ... it has to be open...And it means that I talk to my colleagues. For instance [a colleague] is devising a unit of poetry work to do with [an intern]. It means she and I are talking about poetry work, so it means that we're collaborating more than we would otherwise do. So I think it improves communication, not just between intern and permanent teacher but between the teachers.

Working with interns in departments

In relation to the second theme, departmental arrangements to support the learning of interns, the following issues emerged:

Setting the interns' timetable

In setting interns' timetables, mentors aim to give them experience of a balance of classes of most years and different ability ranges, while taking account of the learning needs of pupils. Mentors are especially conscious about the effects on examination classes, and it is school policy that interns do not engage with these groups.

The nature of mentors' work with interns

The nature of mentors' work changed as interns became increasingly competent and independent. The mentors characterised the Joint Weeks period as one of close contact with the intern where lesson planning, observation and thorough de-briefing of classroom strategies and decisions occurred regularly, citing the timetabled 'mentor period' as essential for this purpose. During the School Weeks period mentors gave increasing responsibility to the interns both in terms of teaching and of their own learning. During the course of the research, intern progress was noticeable; by the time of the final interviews, for example, one had moved on to a role of personally evaluating what the pupils had achieved, suggesting activities to the mentor, planning new work and delivering lessons. While mentors and other teachers limited their observation of lessons at this stage they continued to maintain a presence and to keep in touch with the progress of the class. Timetabled mentor sessions were becoming much more 'open-ended' and dominated by interns' stated needs and concerns. By the time of the Phase 2 interviews with mentors, interns were 'fine-tuning' their material and the structure of their lessons and focusing on things like differentiation and preparing for the reality of teaching life on a full timetable. One mentor added that by now her intern was working more broadly within the framework of the school in order to support the learning of students.

> You know that she's concerned about so and so, that she thinks a certain person's anxious or unhappy about a piece of work or something. And where she suspects there might be an emotional problem or something going on with a pupil, she's going straight to their tutor now to talk to them, or she knows, you know she knows around the staff room who knows that child, who she should talk to. So she is also going to get information on kids, just as I would do if I was wondering what was going on – I would go to a pupil's tutor. So if [intern] mentions it to me, and I say 'Oh you could see her tutor', [intern) says 'I've done that'. So she's following things up with individual pupils. She's using the same systems that we would use.

The nature of interns' work with other departmental staff

From the data it was clear that interns worked in different ways with different teachers within the department. In one department the mentor –

who was also the head of department – while not involving herself in other teachers' classes, would nevertheless discuss with staff the intern's work in all classes. As a consequence, staff in this department knew what the interns were doing and were clear about ways in which they could support them. The other mentor, although an experienced teacher, was new to her teacher educator role and had difficulty in extending the school's commitment to working with student teachers throughout the department. As a consequence she had less knowledge of how the interns were working with other staff and any feedback tended to concentrate on the intern's 'problem-areas'. Support for the mentor's description of these working arrangements came from the intern who asserted that in the absence of appropriate support she would often 'just get on with it' in classes.

Clearly, conversations between interns and a wide range of colleagues were going on in both departments, but there were perceptible differences in the level and nature of the discussions. These perceived differences could, however, be attributed to the rapid progression of one of the interns who by the time of the data collection was in many respects seen as a full member of staff performing well in all classes, taking considerable initiative and working independently.

Monitoring interns' progress

Departments' responses to internship also seemed to influence the extent to which the interns' learning was adequately monitored. As would be expected, mentors were best able to evaluate interns' work with students in relation to their own classes as they felt justified in continuing to observe (in many different ways) and participate throughout the intern's school experience. Monitoring interns' work with colleagues' classes, however, occurred in two distinct ways: the timetabled mentor session was used to question interns and mentors engaged in discussion with relevant colleagues. Mentors, however, seemed inclined to leave the bulk of any concerns raised with others' classes for the intern to discuss directly with those colleagues, giving rise to the possibility that not all mentors were aware of the impact interns were having on the learning of pupils throughout departments.

The discussion above indicates that departmental responses to internship vary greatly. In one department open, detailed and regular discussion characterised the process of monitoring interns' developing classroom skills. Similarly, greater experience of guiding student teacher learning enabled one mentor to be much more specific in verifying her claims about interns' learning and its impact on pupils. The relative inexperience of the other mentor, together with the relative lack of discussion in the department in relation to the intern's progress, may have had implications for the development of the intern's own learning and, in turn, the learning of pupils with whom the intern was associated.

Commentary

A primary concern of schools which engage in initial teacher education must be that their own pupils, as well as the student teachers, should benefit from it. The results reported above, from a school which had such concerns, should be reassuring, although they are clearly not automatically generalisable. The one rule which in our view is generalisable is that the more appropriate the provision made for student teachers' learning, the more certain one can be that pupils will benefit. In the case of the department reported here, in which an inexperienced mentor was working with little support from departmental colleagues, the pupils nonetheless tended to claim that they were benefiting from the presence of the interns, and none thought that their learning was suffering; but in the department where the mentor was working with the collaboration of colleagues to ensure the progressive development of the interns' learning, the pupils were unanimous about the benefits to them, and we as observers were in equally little doubt about these benefits. Schools which take initial teacher education seriously have no need to worry about their pupils.

ITE and the benefits for teachers

It is widely suggested that involvement in school-based ITE can benefit teachers, and in this investigation the school sought to understand more about the nature and extent of such benefits. The research, therefore, was designed to investigate ways in which mentors and other teachers worked with interns, the effect of those interactions on teachers' thinking and practice, and the benefits claimed by the teachers themselves. Three teachers – with teaching experience ranging from five to twenty-five years – were involved in the investigation: one was currently a mentor in the Internship Scheme and the other two were former mentors, one of whom had just taken on the role of professional tutor responsible for internship and the induction of NQTs in the School. Participants were observed working with interns in planning and de-briefing activities and in collaborative classroom work over a 3 month period during S-weeks. Data was collected through in-depth interviews based on these observed interactions.

Each of the three teachers cited distinct areas of development arising from their work with interns. One was more inclined to consider the impact of this engagement on her thinking and practice in the classroom. Another claimed to have developed management skills from her work as mentor which, she explained, had been essential to her recent success in obtaining a promoted role at another school. The third suggested that involvement in initial teacher education had reshaped and re-invigorated her career, enabling her to extend her role within the school whilst remaining grounded in classroom teaching. Notwithstanding these differences, there was a range of claimed benefits common to all three, which can be broadly summarised as:

- developing expertise as a teacher
- developing management skills
- developing thinking about teaching
- greater collegiality
- new dispositions and satisfactions.

These are now discussed in turn.

Developing expertise as a teacher

The teachers talked of two ways in which their knowledge and expertise had been enhanced through their work in internship.

New approaches to facilitating student learning

Student teachers were a ready source of new skills and ideas. One participant suggested that her intern had helped her to focus more clearly on the skills to be developed in classes and that her work with interns had changed 'the way I manage learning'. As a consequence, she had developed more effective strategies for small group work and was more ready and able to withdraw particular students from classes in order to concentrate on their individual learning needs. Another teacher used the distinctive expertise of her interns to 'fill in the gaps' in her own knowledge.

As they became more competent and took on increasing responsibility for classes, interns helped to 'free up' teachers' time. One teacher estimated that after subtracting planning and de-briefing time she gained at least half a day per week much of which was used working with the intern in preparing new materials:

> I was able to dig around and buy a lot of new resources which normally I wouldn't have time to do to the same extent. We were able to have four or five sessions together, planning at various stages, working at drafts, changing things. We were able to trial it with the pupils, both of us mark it, comment on what we'd done and then write the materials together. Now she had time because she's on a reduced timetable. I would never have time to do that unless she had freed up time for me at some place else … we must have spent a good ten hours on that together and she would have spent another five hours out and I would have spent another five hours out. Well, twenty hours just doesn't exist

to write one piece of course work – it just does not exist in a school timetable.

Joint planning, lesson debriefing and continual discussion were the central processes that most often enabled teachers to develop new insights and skills. One of the teachers explained how planning lessons with the intern helped her to reflect on her own teaching:

I now focus on the learning of the pupils in a different way. I consider other possibilities that I wouldn't necessarily consider and the questions I ask myself to get ready to plan with somebody else prompt even further reflection on the teaching...We were talking out aloud about things that all too often can become implicit and assumed. I was having to prepare and think about those things because I am working with an intern.

New understandings about pupils

All three teachers claimed that they gained new insights into their pupil's. In one case the intern acted as a 'sounding board' to discuss the progress and needs of individual pupils. This enabled the teacher to 'understand the dynamics' that characterised a number of 'disaffected' pupils. As a consequence of the intern's insights this teacher was able to relate more effectively to one especially under-motivated girl in a Year 8 class, and the confidence instilled by the intern's thinking and strategies enabled her to undertake interventions in her Year 10 class. Simply having another adult in the classroom freed up the teacher to focus on individuals:

It's really useful to be in your own classroom with your own class, watching someone else teach ... in terms of what you learn about [pupils'] ability to concentrate, about their confidence ... it is important in terms of, for example, [intern's] use of praise during the lesson and you think 'Gosh, she [pupil] really responded to that, that's really useful, I must use that again.

Developing management skills

The development of skills to manage people and resources was a common thread through all of the participants' accounts; indeed, for one of them it was the main benefit from engagement with internship.

There's definite management skills to being a teacher-educator. Managing the interns' time, actually instructing them to provide you with such and such materials at certain times. To be in a certain place at a certain time, to organise meetings with them. Managing their workload, setting timetables for them, telling them how they ought to be spending their energy, particularly about work. The interpersonal skills involved with that are quite tricky, especially if they are under pressure. You've got to be constantly motivating them. Constantly making sure that they are working at a pace that you think is fit – and that means managing your own time efficiently so that you can actually manage theirs.

This teacher claimed that the organisational and communicative skills that enabled her to attain a promoted post came from her work as a mentor. For another of the teachers it was the skills developed through working with interns that proved invaluable in her work with parents. In her words

> I had a very difficult interview with a parent where the goal of the interview was to see the world a little bit more through the teenager's eyes … and she [the parent] was resistant. I don't think that she had fully accepted the difficulties that this pupil might be facing … and all the ramifications of the relationship. And the questioning and the way of talking that one has with an intern where you have a similar resistance or anxiety was invaluable. It was something that I could fall back on.

The same teacher also contended that the skills she had acquired through involvement in internship helped her in working with newly qualified teachers:

> One NQT on my tutor team has not been progressing very well or achieving her tasks. Yesterday she was extremely rude and defensive and I think the skills I've developed through my internship roles like empathising, goal setting and diagnosis have enabled me to get her through.

Developing thinking about teaching

All three teachers claimed that as a consequence of their work with interns they tended to adopt a more critical stance in relation to their own teaching. One of the teachers, for example, had helped the intern focus on his manner in classes and this had encouraged her to challenge her own behaviour:

> It's made me aware because [the intern's] actually changing his own habits which I was identifying. I was thinking 'I really don't think you should sit on the desk. I think you should stand up, don't slouch'. All these things are sending signals. 'Don't keep yourself next to the desk all the time, move around the room. Put your back to the board on occasions, back to the back wall'. And I am saying to myself at the same time, 'Yes, Year 9. You ought to be doing that as well', because, in a sense, you become too comfortable with them.

Similarly,

> When you see an intern who actually doesn't create a good pace in the lesson, it makes you much more aware that you could be doing the same thing. I think in my case, the pace of my lessons sometimes can be a fault of my own teaching, which I quickly see in other people.

Greater collegiality

All participants felt that their involvement with internship created more opportunities to share their practice, thoughts and concerns. Claimed benefits were of two sorts.

Engaging more fully with colleagues

Both the mentor and the professional tutor in particular claimed that working with interns brought them into greater contact with colleagues and obliged them to share decisions and exchange views with other staff. However, it appeared that in many cases the most open and sharing relationships were those between teacher and intern and not between departmental colleagues. Further, much of the dialogue was thought to be temporary and was certainly less common once interns had left the school. One teacher explained:

> What I feel is more frustrating than perhaps sitting at home in isolation is sitting here in isolation working, and feeling that you'd like to try and go in a new direction. But somehow you are in a vacuum and having somebody else to work with – particularly somebody who wants to find out about teaching and wants to find out about learners – is forcing me, all of the time, to re-evaluate the pupils in my classroom, the possibilities for those pupils.

After the intern had completed her school placement this teacher felt as though she was 'grinding to a halt' because of the lack of constructive and analytical input from her colleagues. Internship, however, offered a non-threatening environment for the sharing of expertise and the impact of interns was to keep alive this discussion and sharing.

> I think that when internship is there … we have a focus for our discussion that takes away any sense of criticising each other or appearing to be out of step with other people … it creates a kind of culture where people feel safe. And because interns are at a slightly different learning point to us but are seeing things in a fresh new way, all kinds of previous approaches can almost go on hold. But a bit like any kind of behaviour that you are trying to change, sometimes you get a roll-back and so that when interns are not here, I wonder whether we sometimes roll-back to a more comfortable mode.

Talking about educational matters

Involvement in internship had made one teacher, and many of her colleagues in the department, feel like part of a much larger educational service. Whilst interns were considered to be this teacher's 'main source of contact with broader educational issues' as well as 'the impetus for my thinking about some of them at all', other teachers were able to use the network established by internship to meet subject colleagues at other schools, often 'for the first time ever'. Talking about the subject, engaging widely with colleagues both in schools and at the university, extending understanding through further study and taking more initiative in attempting to guide interns – all were areas of benefit for these participants and factors that led to their developing much richer perspectives as education professionals. One of the teachers claimed that the constant questioning by interns informed her understanding of the National Curriculum and gave rise to a 'much fuller debate about education in general'.

New dispositions and satisfactions

Two areas of benefit were discussed by participants.

Greater experimentation and ambition

All participants claimed that as a consequence of their work with interns they had introduced experimentation into their work and were prepared to risk new approaches. One teacher explained:

> I am providing a lot more variety of teaching methods in the lesson ... Normally I would have about three changes of activity in a sixth form lesson and now I've got about five ... I go into the lessons that I am teaching at the moment with renewed vigour to actually employ lots of these things that I am seeing in terms of teaching.

Working with interns was also seen as a source of motivation:

> If I get tired at the end of a term, what I tend to do is I let them get on with something and I maybe try and sort something out for my next lesson. Just in that five minute slot where they might be doing something – rather than sitting down at the table with them – I might be tempted to actually go and work out where the worksheets are in my filing cabinet for the next lesson. I don't want to do that when I've been watching [the intern] teaching because I'm suddenly aware that really I need to get every ounce of potential out of the children and it encourages you to do that because you can stretch them out much further. Whereas, I think, when you are just in the classroom on your own, teaching, it's very easy to skimp.

One participant now thought of herself as a 'nuisance' in that she was always questioning the assumptions and processes of the department. Further, she claimed that her work with novice teachers had made her constantly seek to devise teaching strategies that would more effectively promote student learning:

> I'm changing the way I manage learning and increasingly question pupils to assess their learning and advancement. This even extends to exam preparation ... I think my involvement with interns has made enormous differences to my outlook and practice as a teacher. I think the biggest thing I've got out of it has had to be the new insights into the nature of learning.

Greater satisfaction

The most experienced of the three participants suggested that her involvement in initial teacher education had enabled her to expand her role within the school whilst remaining firmly grounded in classroom teaching. She was central to the development of an induction programme for NQTs and was keen to extend this into other areas of staff development. Her previous role as mentor and now as professional tutor had exposed her to a range of other experiences and opportunities and for her no other avenue for this sort of growth had previously been possible.

> Because I never wanted to be an administrator … I didn't want to be a senior teacher or deputy head in charge of doing timetables and stuff like that. I wanted to have more of a role in the school but firmly based in classroom teaching.

Finally, for this teacher, engagement with new entrants to the profession was a natural progression.

> If you've been in the profession twenty-five years and you are coming toward the end of the time, it is so natural to be involved with the new people who are coming into it. Obviously it's something that you have got a lot of satisfaction out of in your lifetime although you probably haven't talked about it much or thought about it in those terms. Now you have a chance to naturally renew, almost, your enthusiasm for it as well as know you are doing something useful to bring people into the profession that has meant something to you over many, many years.

Commentary

The rich variety of ways in which these three teachers claimed to have benefited professionally from their work with interns, and the certainty with which they made these claims, seems to us impressive. It also seems potentially important, in that the sustained commitment to initial teacher education by busy teachers will surely depend on much more than the limited financial payments made to schools. Three main questions arise for us. First, how generally do teachers experience such benefits from their engagement in ITE? Second, what conditions or circumstances influence the extent to which the various kinds of benefits are experienced? And third, is it possible and sensible for schools to plan deliberately for such benefits?

Conclusion

Usually, it is people employed in universities who determine agendas for research into initial teacher education; and usually, the focus of these agendas is on factors influencing student teachers' experience and learning. For people working in schools, however, the more problematic aspects of school-based initial teacher education may not be those concerned with its impact on student teachers but rather those concerned with its impact on the schools. Thus it is interesting that, when teachers involved in the

Oxford scheme were invited to raise issues for research, those they raised were about the implications for schools: working relationships in subject departments, implications for NQTs, benefits or losses for students, and professional benefits for teachers. There can be little doubt that teachers are right to emphasise these questions. The implications for schools of accepting major responsibilities for initial teacher education are likely to be profound and very interesting. This chapter has offered some initial insights into what these implications may be.

CHAPTER 7

Mentoring and Continuing Professional Development

Tony Bush, Marianne Coleman, Debbie Wall and John West-Burnham

Introduction

Mentoring has become increasingly important as a mode of professional development in education. Its underlying assumption is that a more experienced colleague can facilitate the professional development of a new teacher or a person new to a particular stage in a career. Almost all definitions of mentoring emphasise the professional development of the mentee. Some also incorporate a notion of personal development.

> Mentoring is a complex, interactive process occurring between individuals of differing levels of experience and expertise which incorporates interpersonal or psycho-social development, career and/or educational development, and socialisation. (Carmin, 1988:9)

This definition suggests that mentoring is a multi-faceted concept, incorporating personal support and the more rigorous notion of professional development leading to enhanced competence. While new professionals, and those adapting to new roles, often welcome a shoulder to cry on, there may be frustration in due course if the mentoring process does not go beyond the personal level to encompass a critical assessment of the mentee's professional practice.

Mentoring has grown in importance in England and Wales, partly as a result of the shift to self-management in schools and colleges. There is a growing recognition that organisational performance depends critically on the selection, development and motivation of staff. The effective induction of new staff, or those adjusting to new roles, is regarded as an important component of the staff development role. Mentoring is an increasingly significant element in the induction process at various stages of a career.

The benefits of mentoring

Mentoring needs to produce benefits for both parties if it is to be a mutually rewarding experience. Mentees at all levels benefit through having legitimate or privileged access to an experienced colleague who can provide support and guidance.

> [The mentee] is learning from the mentor's experience and the mentor's role is to encourage and nurture his or her protégé. Mentors can pass on practical insight derived from experience and can pick up on new ideas and attitudes. They can help their protégés to set realistic expectations and steer them in the right direction as far as their career aspirations are concerned. It can, and should, be a mutually rewarding experience. (Thomson, 1993:111)

As Thomson suggests, mentors may also benefit from mentoring. Indeed, it could be argued that they *must* benefit if they are to invest the time and effort required to perform the role in a meaningful way.

Effective mentoring programmes also produce benefits for the school. Teachers may develop collaborative models of working which enable them to share ideas and problems and enhance the collective competence of the staff.

> [Mentoring] proliferates organizational norms and culture, ensures hard-learned knowledge and skills are transferred to younger colleagues [and] improves the overall performance of the work group. (Chong *et al.*, 1989:21)

Limitations of mentoring

Two factors in particular may serve to limit the potential benefits of mentoring. The first of these is the quality of the match between mentor and mentee. Where there is compatibility between mentor and protégé there is the potential for substantial and often rapid professional growth. Where there are disparities in personal outlook, or professional principles, then the benefits may be limited.

In relation to newly qualified teachers, Bark (1994:87) has shown that there may be advantages in mentees being paired with relatively inexperienced teachers who have a more recent understanding of the difficulties faced by new professionals. Matching with senior staff may discourage protégés who may be reluctant to reveal their limitations to school managers.

> Miss C's mentor was the deputy head teacher. She did not want to let a member of the SMT think she was struggling and turned to a colleague in her second year of teaching. The mentor was aware of this difficulty and also conscious that by being a member of the SMT she had less time to give.

The problem of limited time is the second potential major weakness of mentoring. As Bark (1994) indicates, mentors may be too busy with their other commitments to give sufficient time to their mentees. A cursory approach to mentoring is likely to negate much of the potential benefit. Jacques (1995) reinforces Bark's point by arguing that, while senior teachers have status and expertise, they frequently do not have the time to support their protégés adequately.

These central issues provide the background to the project undertaken in two counties in the East Midlands. This chapter reports empirical research on mentoring at three significant stages: newly qualified teachers, middle managers and headteachers.

Newly qualified teachers and mentoring

Newly qualified teachers (NQTs) are embarking on the first stage of a professional career. They are regarded as competent to teach but their skills are immature and need to be nurtured. A well planned and properly resourced induction programme represents an investment in the professional development of new teachers. Mentoring is increasingly regarded as an important element in that process of induction.

In the authors' research, six schools were selected to represent the range of provision available across two counties: an infant school, junior school, middle school, a high school (11–14) and two secondary schools (11–16 and 11–18). Meetings were held with headteachers and/or professional tutors at each school to inform them about the project and to ascertain what mentoring policies and practices existed. All newly qualified teachers (13) and mentors (11) were interviewed twice during the school year to investigate the nature and development of mentoring for NQTs in their first year of teaching.

Informal and formal practice

In most sample schools, there was no identifiable structure or continuity to mentoring provision.

> It's full of informal mentoring, but we haven't got a formal policy. (headteacher)

Mentoring practices were based along a continuum of formality: from the informal – pretty on the hoof, *ad hoc* conversations over a cup of coffee – to the formal – organised mentoring meetings within a structured framework. In the secondary schools in particular, informal methods prevailed.

Some senior managers saw their involvement with the authors' project as an opportunity to give mentoring 'a test run', with the intention of developing formal strategies in the future. This approach goes some way towards explaining why only one mentor had received any training for the role and why no mentors had received written guidelines from their schools to assist them with their nominated roles.

The absence of a formal mentoring policy in the secondary schools led to fragmented and inconsistent practices across departments, where effective mentoring was dependent on the value placed on it by individual mentors, rather than on direction and leadership from senior management.

> Practice would range from classroom observation and debriefing to informal coffee break chats. I don't think there is an agreed expectation ... there is no explicit formalisation of the mentor role. (secondary school headteacher)

In the secondary schools, mentors did not collaborate on a cross-departmental basis, so were unable to make comparisons with the support available to NQTs in other departments. Also, professional tutors in the two largest secondary schools ran induction programmes for NQTs, but the content of these was not communicated to mentors and they had no input into the sessions.

> I'm not even aware of what happens in the generalised induction programme. (mentor)

A lack of co-ordination between school middle managers or designated mentors and the activities of induction co-ordinators has also been noted by Earley and Kinder (1994: 48).

The absence of formal structure referred to by headteachers and professional tutors was reiterated by NQTs and mentors during the first round of interviews, particularly by those from the two large secondary schools.

> To be honest, I'm not really *au fait* with how the school's mentoring system is structured. (mentor)

> Certainly, within the department, I haven't been told or instructed that I've got a particular mentor .. I didn't know we had one. I don't think it's a school policy to have one yet. (NQT)

NQTs were often left to ask for advice as problems arose and this superficial level of support restricted the opportunity to gain insight into the pedagogic skills of the mentor.

> It's tended towards crisis management rather than looking at the reasons behind issues ... to be just dealing with the pupils concerned, rather than helping me to develop new strategies. (NQT)

During the first interviews, some of the NQTs and mentors argued against the rigidity of a formal system of arranged meetings and for 'an informal exchange agreement'.

> It seems to be pretty informal at the moment ... which is how I like it. I don't really like being pinned down ... I'm much happier being given a bit of passing guidance when I need it. (NQT)

However, this initial confidence in informal mentoring had all but dissipated by the second round of interviews.

> I feel like it's sink or swim at times ... I think I could have done with some more structured support ... I can see that now. You can't rely on *ad hoc* meetings because they disappear. You've no time. (NQT)

The experiences of the NQTs in the one school that did provide regular mentoring meetings, substantiate West-Burnham's thesis (1993:133) that a formal mentoring relationship in structural terms does not have to be formal in interpersonal terms. Here, the two NQTs stressed that much of the success of their mentoring programme was 'because we get on as personalities' and because there was a good professional relationship with both the mentor and headteacher. This school appeared to have achieved a successful balance between a formal structure and informal interpersonal relationships.

> I wouldn't want to change anything or do anything differently. At the end of this year I just feel really happy that this mentoring process won't really stop. I don't feel really that there's been an official mentoring process, it's just been what happens. I haven't had any problems, it's been super. I couldn't have wished for a better start really. (NQT)

Managers as mentors

All newly qualified teachers in our sample were allocated a mentor by senior managers although there was a problem in disseminating this information to some mentors and NQTs.

> I wondered who it was after about three weeks. (NQT)

> Nobody's told me what my role's supposed to be. (mentor)

Eight of the eleven mentors in the sample had management responsibilities and at the secondary schools all but one of the seven mentors was the new teacher's head of department. The role of mentor was often 'assumed' by the head of department: a new label to attach to his or her normal duties as subject specialist with responsibility for new teachers.

> It's something I've done for a long time without having been called a mentor.

It was also apparent that use of the term 'mentor' varied from school to school. In the words of a secondary headteacher, 'they (HoDs) wouldn't know what a mentor is ... the word "mentor" is new.'

NQTs, on the other hand, distinguished between head of department and mentor, rather than synthesising the two roles. Their perceptions of the mentor role and their expectations of the mentoring process were often informed by their experiences during initial teacher training, including recollections of structured partnership programmes. In this respect, the authors' research supports Southworth's view (1994:10) that teachers new to the profession may have more familiarity with the mentoring 'process' than the mentors themselves.

> I've viewed him as head of department rather than a mentor. Maybe he's not enough of my personal mentor. I get the benefit out of him as I would out of any head of department, I think. Nothing more at this stage. (NQT)

There was also evidence that the management status of mentors and their level of experience in the classroom could make them less approachable with problems, reinforcing the point made by Bark (1994) that relatively inexperienced teachers may be more suitable as mentors (see page 122).

> We just haven't had that close a relationship. I think partly because he's head of department, I'm keen to be seen to be doing a good job. Perhaps I find it harder to talk to him for that reason.

Time to mentor

A further difficulty with the manager/mentor dichotomy was that the demands of management often restricted the time available for mentoring (Shaw 1992: 77). New teachers expressed some frustration about this.

> I think perhaps the mentor should be somebody with experience, but not somebody in such a position that they don't have time to give you, because time is what I need from people like her. (NQT with senior manager mentor)

The new teachers were sympathetic to mentors' workloads and avoided approaching them at times they deemed inappropriate, but this inevitably meant that some issues were never raised for discussion.

> It's that, 'Will I ask? Do I ask?' type of thing. 'Are they too busy? Oh, I'll leave it.' (NQT)

The need for time to be available in order for mentoring practice to be effective has been noted in much of the previous research in this area (Earley and Kinder, 1994:65, Dart and Drake, 1994:23). It is therefore unsurprising that this was the key area of concern for mentors and NQTs.

> She's not mentor material, she just doesn't have the time. (NQT)

The lack of time for mentoring was due to several factors, the most frequently cited being that no time-tabled space had been allocated for meetings of mentor and NQT. These constraints, where typically mentoring was located in 'any time we can grab', were inextricably linked to the lack of formal mentoring provision. Mentors and NQTs were clear that the only way to alleviate the problem was to provide adequate structures from the outset.

I really do think that if the induction of NQTs is being done properly, it's got to be timetabled. There's got to be time set aside which is yours with that particular person. That has got to be built in from the start and it's not built in. You end up with a situation where the thing has just drifted and it's a school where the more you take on, the more difficult it becomes to do things and you've got to say to yourself, 'Well, will something give?' (mentor, HoD)

Other views expressed about time constraints included:

- lack of non-contact time
- non-contact time of mentor and NQT not coinciding
- little or no reduction in workload of NQTs compared with experienced colleagues
- the need to provide cover for mentoring during directed time
- form tutor responsibilities and other commitments which were often being met for the first time by the NQT.

Under such circumstances, mentoring could 'just fizzle out'.

There are always lots of pressures and mentoring is one of the things that can be squeezed. I think that's one of the problems. (mentor)

These views illustrate the point, made in the introduction, that lack of time is a significant potential weakness of mentoring.

The benefits of mentoring

Wall and Smith (1993:19) have listed the benefits that NQTs, trained mentors and the teaching profession generally derive from mentoring. The benefit most comparable with the project findings is 'having someone to talk to', which was cited by the majority of NQTs during interview.

The benefit is that there is someone there who you can talk to; who has been at the school more than a couple of years; who hopefully can give you realistic guidelines as to what you might be achieving; who knows many of the pupils; who knows the school's strategies and routines. That clearly is helpful.

New teachers derived benefit from the advice of their mentors as experienced practitioners and as informants on the procedures of their schools. The benefits of mentoring also included: having someone who would listen and act as a 'sounding board'; who offered guidance and reassurance; who was non-judgmental and who could admit that they were fallible, that 'some of the problems that they're having, we're all having to a different degree'.

NQTs also valued constructive, critical feedback from their mentors about their progress and the opportunity to be observed and to observe other colleagues teaching.

128

> It's nice to either be told to buck your ideas up, or get a pat on the back, rather than be just left to it. (NQT)

However, as we noted in the introduction, the process provided benefits for the mentor as well as the new teacher.

> She's taught me a lot and that's been good.

> We've actually learnt together.

> He's caused me to examine my teaching as well.

> It's professional development right the way through.

Mentoring was variously described by mentors as 'a learning partnership','a two way interaction', 'for mutual support' and 'of benefit to both of us'.

Mentors valued the opportunity to reflect on and question their own subconscious practice, to share new ideas and developments that NQTs brought to teaching and, at primary level, to learn about the NQT's specialist subject area. According to Stanulis (1994:37), by studying their own practice in this way, teacher mentors 'can begin to realise the importance of making ordinarily tacit knowledge explicit to novices'. This view was reflected in comments to one of the researchers.

> It does challenge the way that you teach and the way that you think about teaching, because you have to actually have thought through what you do and then analyse why you do it and decide whether it is right or not, before you pass it on to somebody else. That does clarify your own ideas. (mentor)

Shaw (1992:76) also cites the improved career prospects offered by the mentor role as one of the benefits for individual teachers. One of the mentors in the authors' sample made a direct link between mentoring and the advancement of his own career.

> It's obviously something else you can put on your c.v. and something else that you can learn from. It's useful for when hopefully you move further up the career ladder. I can see there are advantages for me.

He also cited the benefits for the whole school.

> If you don't provide the support then the children don't get taught as effectively as they can do. The more constructive you can be with the support, the more the learning of the children is likely to improve.

Mentoring and teacher development

The lack of systematic mentoring processes made it difficult to investigate mentoring practice and development. Interview questions related to when and where meetings took place and their frequency and subject matter, did not stand easily alongside such comments as

You definitely meet when you can, *ad hoc*, dinner times and things like that. (NQT)

Mentoring was highly valued by new teachers and their mentors, but there was agreement that it needs to receive wider recognition and acknowledgement at senior management levels if practice is to be improved and developed.

Involvement with the project raised awareness of mentoring in the schools, but for most, mentoring practice was still fragmented at the end of the year.

There's a lot of talk about mentoring, but nothing has ever actually been set up. There's all these good intentions, but nothing has been followed through.' (NQT)

The notion of structured programmes providing the opportunity for formal meetings of mentoring partners was cited as the way forward. As one mentor said.

I'd like to see it done in a professional way, rather than in an *ad hoc* way.

By the end of the research period there were signs that two schools were developing commitment to mentoring in their institutions. One school invited all teachers to a meeting with a view to formulating a school policy on mentoring. In another school, understanding of the relationship between mentoring and the professional development of teachers was enhanced when mentors and NQTs produced a booklet on mentoring and completed personal professional profiles together.

The opportunities for new teachers to reflect on career and professional development were few when time was not allocated for mentoring. However, the authors' research does support the findings of Kelly *et al.*, (1992:179) that mentoring is not only applicable to those in their first year of teaching, but can play an important part in the professional development of more senior colleagues too.

I see mentoring as really a part of the continuing professional support and development of staff; it's an element within that as a whole. Really my argument would be that to look at NQTs as a separate entity is wrong and that mentoring should be a continuing process within the profession...Everybody needs guidance and support, and the establishment needs to show that by creating a structure that gives it. (mentor)

This philosophy underpins the approach to mentoring adopted in the case study schools featured in the next section.

Mentoring and middle management

The decision to include middle managers in the research project grew out of an awareness that, although they comprise one of the most significant cohorts in schools, they have not yet been included in official mentoring programmes. It was therefore decided to examine what contribution, if any, the concept of mentoring makes to understanding the role of middle managers and their relationship with headteachers and senior staff.

Torrington and Weightman (1989) defined heads of department and pastoral team leaders as the 'neglected roles' in school management. They identified lack of role clarity, inconsistent perceptions of the place of middle management and limited formalised training and development, as key inhibitors to the effectiveness of these functions. This latter point was reinforced by the School Teacher Review Board (1993) which highlighted concerns about the effectiveness of school management:

- the failure of some schools to translate curriculum and pastoral policies into effect
- middle managers who do not recognise or exercise their managerial role or are not used in that way by heads
- confusion between administration and management with an undue emphasis on the former.

The lack of structured and integrated support for middle managers was a significant feature of the research carried out by Earley and Fletcher-Campbell (1989:103).

> It was ... noted that although some departments *could* operate effectively with little or no support from senior staff and/or the education authority, the chances of departments and their staffs developing to their *full potential* were slim.

This issue of support is the main focus of this part of the chapter.

Initial interviews were conducted in a primary school, an 11–14 secondary school and a 14–18 upper school. The preliminary responses from the three schools showed that mentoring was not formalised but was understood and seen as a desirable component of working relationships between senior and middle managers. Interviewees placed great stress on the importance of good interpersonal relationships and emphasised the problems caused by hierarchical relationships and the lack of time. There was a consensus about the positive benefits of linking mentoring with appraisal.

Two of the three schools were subsequently included in the substantive phase of the research. The primary school had a headteacher plus twelve teachers but no deputy head. When the most recent holder of the post retired the decision was taken not to reappoint a deputy but to appoint three team leaders (infants, lower juniors and upper juniors). The secondary school is an 11–14 school with head, deputy and 38 teachers. The management issue in this school was the movement away from an hierarchical, dependency culture in which the headteacher was perceived as the sole arbiter to one of high levels of delegation of responsibility and the encouragement of interdependent working.

The issue of defining middle management (always a nebulous term) was resolved by the decision to regard the team leaders in the primary school, and year heads and heads of department in the secondary school, as middle managers. This coincides with the nomenclature used by Earley and Fletcher-Campbell (1989).

This study examines the following topics: the status of mentoring, criteria for successful mentoring, barriers to mentoring and mentoring and appraisal.

The status of mentoring

The term mentoring was not generally in use in the schools but the concept was widely understood.

> I think it means a continuous process of support, consultation, drawing out, target setting, renewing and reflecting. (secondary school headteacher)

> It's about sharing, problem solving and developing a common approach. (primary school headteacher)

What is significant here is the emphasis on a positive and supportive approach which is reflected in the views of staff.

> I suppose I would see a mentor as a fairly experienced practitioner who was trying to share some of the things they had discovered – in the hope that this would be a supportive process. (secondary school year head)

There was a clear recognition of the importance of the mentor having greater experience, expertise or knowledge.

> She (the head) knows a lot and shares it. I've copied a lot of her practice – picking out the bits I like. (primary school team leader)

> The management team is constantly being taught by the head. (primary school team leader)

Both heads saw the mentoring relationship as a crucial means of developing consistent practice, of 'telling stories' or providing a model. The primary school management meeting (head and team leaders) was seen by all involved as a major opportunity for mentoring, with the head using explicit strategies and then asking

> How do you think you could get your teams to work like this? (primary school headteacher)

However, as with NQT mentoring, the process was often informal, happening 'anytime, anywhere'.

Mentoring was not formalised in either school in the sense of being defined in school policies, resourced with time or codified in job descriptions. There was no systematic training for mentors or mentees although clear links were drawn with appraisal. The overwhelming impression in both schools was that

> Informal mentoring is taking place all the time. (secondary school deputy head)

> Putting mentoring on the agenda in a formal sense is a dead duck! (secondary school headteacher).

Criteria for successful mentoring

In both schools there was an emphasis on the importance of interpersonal relationships and the availability of the mentor with a minimal emphasis on hierarchy.

> I do feel I can say what I want – I always feel I have been listened to and valued. (secondary school year head)

Listening and feedback were the skills in mentors that were most expected and appreciated.

> I can be open and honest because I feel secure. (primary school team leader)

The skill of attending, i.e. the complete commitment of the mentor, emerged as a significant factor in the effectiveness of discussions between mentor and mentee and in terms of the credibility of the mentor.

> I am never blasted out or undermined, she listens, takes me seriously – but there is often a lot of laughter. (primary school team leader)

> She listens, tunes in to the hidden agenda and knows when to intervene...She has interpersonal skills of a highly developed nature. (secondary school head of department)

The mentors recognised the importance of their behaviour in this respect.

> I must make sure that the person feels on top – making them feel comfortable is vital. (secondary school deputy head)

It was consistently stated that formal hierarchical relationships were alien to an effective mentoring relationship. In the secondary school the head and deputy used mentoring as a specific strategy to reduce hierarchical dependence by providing support for autonomous action.

> Hierarchy can be a very negative force when working for school improvement. (secondary school deputy head)

In the primary school frequent reference was made to the need for relationships between adults to serve as a model for relationships between adults and children.

> A relaxed and comfortable relationship is important – we must work together on the same principles as we work with children. (primary school headteacher)

This lack of formality and structure was reinforced by views on the availability of the mentor.

> I just go straight in and we talk it through. (secondary school head of department)

> I make contact with everybody every morning. (primary school headteacher)

References were made to a 'constant dialogue', 'getting rid of us and them', 'day-to-day discussion and dialogue'. In both schools, senior staff were constantly prepared to assume the role of mentor – it was fundamental to their perceptions of their role even though it was not formally codified. This had a clear impact on the way that middle managers had come to perceive their relationship with their departmental colleagues.

> It's what is most important to the teachers that matters, it's what they want – direct practical help and support. (secondary school year head).

Barriers to mentoring

As we noted earlier, the major barrier to the development of an effective mentoring relationship is the perceived lack of time.

> The thing that really holds me back is a substantial teaching commitment. (secondary school deputy head)

Both headteachers had clearly made a commitment to be available to their middle managers. The frustrations and concern emerged in the inability of middle managers to replicate the relationship with their colleagues.

> It is important that we are available and it must be informal and this is not always possible. (primary school team leader)

Respondents identified the barriers to effective mentoring as poor personal relationships, an emphasis on status and hierarchical control, and limited availability of mentors.

Mentoring and appraisal

In both schools the process of mentoring was perceived to be an important component of leadership and management. However, there was a very real feeling that any attempt to formalise, institutionalise or systemise it would be counterproductive.

> Much of the mentoring that goes on is instructive; it focuses on positive reinforcement and valuing and the whole idea is to widen thought processes. (secondary school deputy head)

However, there was some concern that this level of informality could be counter productive, echoing the view expressed earlier (p.121) that the mentoring process may lack 'rigour'.

> Informal discussion can lead to bland responses – it can become too friendly, too nice. (secondary school head of department)

Both schools had gone some way to using appraisal as a means of structuring the relationship.

> Appraisal nudges us gently to make sure that things happen. (primary school team leader)

> The appraisal cycle is a useful discipline – it is an entitlement and ensures a minimal level of contact. (secondary school headteacher)

This view of appraisal was expressed in the context of the open access and continuous review described above. Perhaps the most significant feature to emerge about the nature of mentoring in middle management was the emphasis on professional learning with frequent references to 'review and reflection', 'modelling' and 'disseminating good practice.' All participants valued the evolution of a mentoring relationship with their headteacher.

The linkage between appraisal and mentoring is defined by Trethowan (1991:127).

> Managers in schools, as elsewhere, are under pressure to produce results and to monitor their team … The existence of a mentor system allows other senior staff in school to help to advise, coach and develop specified teachers, thus sharing in the work of staff development.

This suggests that if appraisers become mentors who engage in coaching, the chances of bringing about significant change in practice are substantially enhanced. If the other components of successful appraisal schemes are added to the equation – the generation of individual targets through the school development plan and the existence of criteria for effective practice – then it is possible to see how mentoring could act as an agent for enhancing the effectiveness of middle managers.

The mentoring of headteachers

The school is the context for mentoring both NQTs and middle managers. Mentors and mentees work in the same professional environment and part of the process relates to imparting aspects of school culture. For new headteachers mentoring cannot operate in this way. Mentors usually know little about the new head's school and this inevitably influences the nature of the mentoring process.

The School Management Task Force (SMTF) recognised the importance of preparing and supporting new headteachers.

> The headteacher plays a highly significant role in school management, being

both focus and pivot at the centre of decision-making. Preparing, inducting and developing headteachers is a major responsibility of the education service. (SMTF, 1990:3)

The SMTF recommended the development of mentoring programmes as part of the induction of new headteachers. Funding has been made available for the training of mentors, and to allow cover to be brought in for time spent on the mentoring process.

Mentoring is a significant feature of the training of school principals in the USA.

We believe that the use of mentors to assist leaders is a powerful tool that may be used to bring about more effective practice in schools. Structured mentor programs are effective strategies to help individuals move into leadership roles more smoothly. (Daresh and Playko, 1992:146)

In the USA, and in Singapore, mentoring has featured as part of a broader programme of pre-service training, whereas in Britain specific headship training is not required before appointment. Mentoring may therefore play a particularly important role in the British context, being regarded 'as a substitute for training rather than forming part of it' (Bush, 1995:3).

The authors' research involved seven headteacher and mentor pairs from primary and secondary phases of education in both counties. One of these pairs was cross-phase, a primary head mentoring a secondary head. Each pair was interviewed twice to gauge their reactions to the process of mentoring near the beginning of the first year of headship and towards the end of that year. In addition, meetings of mentoring pairs were observed, and, in some cases, logs of meetings completed by the respondents helped to supplement interview and observation data.

The nature of the relationship

Heads and mentors were asked to consider the following alternatives as conceptualisations of the mentoring relationship: expert-novice, peer-support, co-counselling, coaching and socialisation.

Mentoring of one headteacher by another was generally seen as *peer support*. Most participants were quick to identify that the mentoring of one headteacher by another is of a different order to the mentoring of an NQT by a more experienced colleague. The new head and the mentor were seen as: 'two people of equal standing'. It was also recognised that

The mentor has had areas of experience that the new head does not have … I have areas of experience he did not have. (new head)

I am learning from X. It is a two-way relationship. (mentor)

However, in one case a head clearly regarded mentoring as more positive than peer support.

I don't feel any of the pressures, the negative support that peer support sometimes can provide. When you're talking with a peer you sometimes feel defensive about what you're doing or you're not willing to acknowledge ignorance.

For another head, the concept of *expert-novice*, or at least the importance of the greater headship experience of the mentor, was the key to the relationship and

Peer support is what I'm getting in the informal network between the cluster group of heads.

The expert-novice conceptualisation was at least partially accepted by some of the new heads but firmly rejected by the mentors, who tended to stress the point that the two heads operate in different contexts.

The new head is expert and will be an expert in their own school, The mentor is not an expert in that school, but may be an expert in their own school. (mentor)

There were differences of view about the validity of *counselling* as a way of conceptualising the relationship.

Mentoring does have elements of counselling, notably in listening and in empathising with the mentee. (mentor)

Counselling is personal and involves a willingness to bare the soul. Mentoring is professional. (new head)

There may be a counselling element to the early stages of the relationship, which changes with the growing experience of the new head.

Perhaps counselling is the first phase and the peer support is the second bit. (new head)

Generally the concept of *coaching* was rejected. The training undertaken by the majority of mentors in our sample does not include the notion of coaching, nor does it include the possibility of observation or of the mentor shadowing the new head. The stress is on listening, exploring feelings and encouraging reflection in the new head (Grubb Institute 1993). Even where mentor training does include elements like work shadowing, it does not seem to be generally accepted as an important part of mentoring headteachers in England and Wales.

Although a good many mentors had received some training in work shadowing, in practice comparatively few of them carried this out. (Bolam *et al.*, 1994:18)

The concept of *socialisation* was not considered important to the understanding of mentoring, and where mentors and new heads recognised socialisation as part of the relationship, it was narrowly interpreted as the introduction of the new headteacher to others in the area, who might prove to be useful contacts.

The impact of mentoring

If mentoring for headteachers is seen as part of induction, and implicitly part of their management training, it is likely that the impact of mentoring will feed through into aspects of the management of the school.

> Management development is about the development of managers, the development of management and its practice and must relate closely to the organisation and its development. (SMTF, 1990:8)

However, as we noted earlier, mentoring has been identified as providing both career and psychosocial support (Kram, 1983; O'Neill *et al.*, 1994). For our mentors and new headteachers, the impact of mentoring was experienced primarily in relation to personal qualities and skills, but inevitably such reflection and development were seen to have an impact on the management of the school.

> I think initially it's likely to be about my personal skills ... I would have thought that the kind of time line would be, personal qualities in schools, moving into the management structures. (new head)

The mentors generally saw the impact of mentoring as being more personal.

> I would say it's better not to know about the school. What is the only thing of interest is what the new head's perceptions are, because that's what you're working with. So I would say it's about relationships ... and the personal.

However, as the year progressed there was a more overt recognition by heads of the impact of mentoring on management.

> Directly and indirectly he has had an impact on decisions made within the school. I had to be comfortable they were my decisions even though they were a product of joint discussion.

> As a result of working with her, the things I was wanting to do have been more polished maybe, better planned ... it's highly tied up with personal skills.

In the end it may be impossible to separate personal from school issues.

> He has identified personal targets he wants to develop. But alongside that, new heads inevitably make an impact on structure and processes. Indeed it is the best opportunity new heads have to do that. (mentor)

The benefits of mentoring

In the first few months of headship, the value of the mentoring process was identified as giving the new head the opportunity to talk to another professional; the mentor was seen as being a 'respondent' to issues raised by the mentee. This finding also emerged from the evaluation of the SMTF pilot mentoring scheme which identified one of the most important role components of the mentors as being a 'catalyst/sounding board' (Bolam *et al.*, 1994:7)

Headship is an isolated position, and it is not possible to discuss every issue with the senior management team. Mentoring gave an opportunity for discussion that would not occur in another context.

> At the level of headship it is different, it is a plunge into the unknown. You cannot ask for help. Therefore you need someone with whom you can speak in total confidence and bounce ideas off, and who you can trust to give impartial and objective advice ... You are able to divulge weaknesses and apprehensions in a way that you cannot elsewhere. (new head)

In addition mentoring has the advantage of being a structured and sanctioned activity.

> It provides me with formalised, almost permission-giving, opportunities to talk through issues and talk through my thoughts with another professional. (new head)

The majority of new heads and mentors summed up the main purpose of mentoring as support: 'primarily a support mechanism', 'peer support', 'support to new colleagues'. In particular, they emphasised the continuing support of a professional in whom they have trust and confidence.

A related benefit was acknowledged to be the provision of the opportunity for reflection which allowed 'the opportunity for constructive analysis', and the ability to formulate: 'a sharper definition of what heads do'. The importance of listening, and the encouragement of reflection in the mentoring relationship, was bolstered by the mentor training which most mentors had attended. This had stressed their function as helping new heads 'find' their new role.

> A mentor is not someone who knows the answers but someone who makes the heads build up a picture of their own school – the school they have in their mind. (mentor)

In the second round of interviews, there appears to have been a change in the way that mentors and new heads saw the purpose and benefit of the relationship. There was a general agreement that the purpose of mentoring was peer support. The need for 'a shoulder to cry on', a sentiment expressed by several new heads in the first interviews, had disappeared by the end of the year, and there was less mention by the mentors of 'developing the vision of the school', possibly reflecting the progress and increasing confidence of the new heads.

Mentors generally recognised that 'peer support is really a two way contract'. They are well aware of potential benefits for themselves as mentors, particularly when opportunities for professional development are limited.

Staff get opportunities, but there are few for heads, other than those just for information. The development involved is one of its biggest pluses.

Mentors also gain from the relationship. Direct benefit was experienced from the opportunity to learn from the expertise of the new headteacher.

> The head I mentored last year taught me an awful lot about the way she deals with parents and governors. (mentor)

Mentors valued the opportunity of taking on a role that allowed reflection, finding this a contrast to their normal range of activities.

> I find it very good to have to sit back and be the less dominant person in the relationship, and actually give space to somebody else.

Most mentors expressed an altruistic wish to support new heads, recognising that they would have liked such support themselves when they were new headteachers.

The limitations of mentoring

As we noted earlier, lack of time can limit the value of mentoring. This problem was the one most frequently identified by both mentors and new heads.

> Such a shortage of time these days to do everything that you need to do, that's the only disadvantage. (mentor)

Effective mentoring also depends on a good match between mentor and mentee. Several respondents felt that the relationship would have been impossible if they had not been able to establish a common view on mentoring and its purpose, and indeed if they had not been able to establish a good personal relationship. In all cases the mentor and new headteacher envisage a continuing relationship, although normally on the basis of being part of the local network, or meeting socially. Only in one case will the more formal relationship be continued.

The potential for difficulties over confidentiality was indicated, including the difficulty for the mentor of knowing when to pass on information about problems divulged in the context of mentoring.

> If, as a mentor you had, at some point of the mentoring relationship, substantial concerns about the way in which the person you were working with was going about things, or even concerns for their welfare, you could really be faced with some very difficult decisions to make.

The new headteachers suggested that there is a risk of dependence on the mentor, and of allowing the mentor to exert too much influence.

> The extent to which the mentor's influence clouded my objectivity. One concern could be. 'Was I doing this or was the mentor doing it?'

New heads also identified problems arising from differences in the background of the mentors and heads. In the one case of cross-phase mentoring, their differing experiences meant that the relationship did not develop.

> Initially I did not think that cross-phase mentoring would be a problem, but I am not so sure any more … At root, issues of scale in management are important. (new head, secondary)

We noted earlier that the development of the mentoring relationship may mean that the needs of mentees change from pure support and a 'shoulder to cry on' to one which is more challenging. One new head, whilst recognising the benefits to be gained ('it saved my sanity') also felt that mentoring

> Needed to be more rigorous and developmental, that the relationship might have benefited from more rigour.

Indeed mentoring for headteachers has been described as a 'process of peer support which is intended to get beyond anecdote and sympathy into development'. (Welsh Joint Education Committee, quoted by Bolam *et al.*, 1994:3)

Conclusion

The research reported in this chapter relates to three important stages of professional development in education. All teachers need a process of induction at the start of their careers and mentoring can help to ease the mentee's transition from student to qualified professional. Most teachers subsequently take on additional responsibilities, perhaps as heads of departments or subject co-ordinators, and mentoring may be valuable as new and unfamiliar tasks are added to the core classroom role. Some professionals may become headteachers and mentoring can make a significant contribution in the early formative period in this senior position.

The authors' research shows that mentoring can be a significant element in the professional development of teachers. The opportunity to receive guidance from a more experienced colleague may help to reduce the anxiety often experienced during the 'apprenticeship' phase of a new or extended career. Our findings suggest that effective mentoring reduces professional isolation, provides support and feedback on performance and gives confidence to mentees during a period of change and uncertainty.

It is evident, too, that the benefits may not be confined to mentees. The mentors in all phases of the research refer to their gains from the process, including re-appraisal of their own practice prompted by the new ideas of the protégé. The school itself may also benefit if a climate of mentoring extends beyond the formal 'pairs' to include other relationships between staff and with pupils. Berrill (1992: 166–67), a secondary deputy head, refers to the impact on his own school.

There is no doubt that observing the growing competence of a colleague has a corresponding training effect for the mentor. If this effect is multiplied within an institution and the mentors are networked in some way it has the potential for powerful institutional development ... it is slowly enhancing our professional ethos.

However, much depends on the status of mentoring in the school. In some schools, the notion of mentoring is weakly defined and appears to have little impact beyond the immediate relationship. Our findings show considerable uncertainty about the nature of the mentor role; this is exacerbated by a lack of time to develop the relationship properly. Mentors do not understand what is expected of them and mentees are not always clear about when they are entitled to 'be mentored'. The potential benefits of mentoring are not being realised in these schools.

In some schools, however, a mentoring culture is developing which goes beyond the sponsored initiatives for newly qualified teachers and new heads to influence the climate of professional development. The two case study schools show that mentoring can be used to develop middle managers when it is actively promoted by the head and senior staff.

It is possible that mentoring cultures will become more widespread as a result of the two major initiatives discussed in this chapter. Newly qualified teachers who benefit from mentoring may adopt this approach in their subsequent dealings with colleagues, and there is evidence that mentoring influences the style of management adopted by new heads.

Mentoring is now well established in many schools but there is little clarity about the nature of the relationship. Several different concepts have been advanced in the literature, including counselling and coaching. These notions have gained some support from the empirical evidence but no dominant model has emerged.

In the introduction we referred to the tension between the supportive role of the mentor and the need for a more rigorous approach leading to professional development. Many of the participants in the research regard support as an essential element of mentoring. New teachers, or those embarking on a new phase of their career, often feel insecure and need support from a more experienced colleague who understands the demands of that career stage.

Effective support requires mentors to develop counselling skills. Clutterbuck (1992:13) regards counselling as one of 'the key roles of mentoring'. The concept of counselling has gained some empirical support in the authors' research.

[The mentor's] work is like that of a counsellor, she listens and makes me reflect. (new principal)

Somebody who follows you closely and supports you, watches you and helps you to develop professionally. (NQT)

The last comment suggests that counselling can lead to professional development, a point also raised by Berrill (1992:166). He refers to the mentor as 'professional guardian, counsellor and friend' but adds that this description 'needs to be developed if mentoring is to be adequately conceptualised and taken seriously as a professional activity'.

Field (1994:67) also emphasizes that mentoring should go beyond support to facilitate professional growth: 'There is a distinction between social support that puts newcomers at ease and professional support that advances knowledge and practice'.

The participants in the NQT phase of the research wanted 'constructive, critical, feedback' on their progress while one new head said that the relationship 'might have benefited from more rigour'. It is evident from our work that both support *and* rigour are required if the mentoring process is to promote professional development. This finding supports the work of Elliott and Calderhead (1993:172) who advocate a two-dimensional model of challenge and support to enhance professional growth.

An alternative conception of mentoring is that of coaching. Clutterbuck (1992:9) refers to coaching as one of 'the core skills' of mentoring while Finn (1993:152) also uses the coaching analogy: 'Mentors act as coaches to help develop protégés' skill and capabilities. The purpose is to prepare the protégé for their future'.

The notion of coaching is reinforced by the findings of Joyce and Showers (1980) and Showers (1985). Wallace (1990:21–22) summarises their main points:

> Coaching in the job situation by colleagues who have also received training is particularly powerful ... Coaching implies that teachers observe each other and give mutual feedback to see how far the skills have been practised; they examine the appropriate use of the strategy; and they engage in collaborative problem solving and action planning sessions.

Wallace's reference to 'training' is significant. Most of the headteacher mentors in our research had undertaken a structured training programme and were generally confident about their mentor role. However, almost all of the NQT mentors had received no formal training and this contributed to a lack of clarity about their role.

Wallace's emphasis on coaching and feedback receives some empirical support from our research. Some NQTs welcomed the opportunity to be observed while the work on middle management and headteachers suggested that coaching could bring about significant changes in practice.

Kram (1983) emphasises the dynamic or changing nature of mentoring, stressing that it changes over time, as the relationship matures. At certain points it might include elements of coaching and counselling but the relationship is individual, depending as much on the personal characteristics of mentor and protégé as on any predetermined notions of the nature of the relationship. Mentoring is an elusive concept which resists simplistic 'labels'.

The authors' research confirms that the mentor relationship works very well for some. The support of an experienced colleague is welcome, particularly in the initial stages of a new career phase, but a more rigorous approach, involving challenge and feedback, is required to achieve meaningful professional development.

CHAPTER 8

Mentoring: Challenges for the Future

Donald McIntyre and Hazel Hagger

We are pleased to note that none of the chapters of this book has sought to present a great success story about mentoring. Contrary to the naïve assumptions of such right wing ideologues as O'Hear (1988) and Lawlor (1990), neither teaching nor teacher education are simple enterprises; and since as yet we have had only a few years' experience of school-based initial teacher education, it is inevitable that we should still be at an early stage in clarifying its problems and possibilities. We are certainly not ready yet to generate useful research-based models of school-based ITE and its implications. Our understandings are however developing and the six research projects reported in this book have all offered valuable new information and perspectives to add to that understanding. It remains for us to bring together in this chapter some of the insights of the different authors within the framework of the several themes which we indicated in our introductory chapter. As our title suggests, our aim is to offer challenges – suggestions to be tried or questions to be answered – which we hope will be helpful to policy makers, practitioners and researchers.

The concept of mentoring

In their introduction to Chapter 7, Tony Bush and his Leicester colleagues suggest that

> mentoring is a multi-faceted concept incorporating personal support and the more rigorous notion of professional development leading to enhanced competence.

In their conclusion to the chapter, however, they also note that

> mentoring is now well established in some schools but there is little clarity about the nature of the relationship. Several different concepts have been advanced in the literature, including counselling and coaching. These notions have gained some support from the empirical evidence but no dominant model has emerged.

Which of these two perspectives should we emphasize? Following the first of these suggestions we could see mentoring as a complex but widely applicable idea, some aspects of which may be neglected in some contexts and some in others. In that case a fruitful way forward would probably be to think about what we can learn about mentoring in schools from mentoring in other contexts, and what useful lessons can be learned for mentoring in different school contexts by comparing effective practices in each. The aim would be to elaborate and refine a generic concept of mentoring.

Following the second of the above suggestions, we might be more pessimistic about the value of such a generic concept. It might be that the widespread use of the term 'mentoring' is possible only because a lack of clarity about what it means allows it to be used to describe very different kinds of roles and relationships, each perhaps appropriate in a different context. In that case we should need to concentrate our energies on clarifying what we think is appropriate for each type of context, and on firmly distinguishing it from the roles and relationships appropriate for other contexts.

The Leicester team are surely right to imply that there is merit in both these perspectives. Their own sympathies, however, tend fairly clearly towards the first of them. We in contrast have tended to favour the second alternative, describing conceptions of mentoring imported to initial teacher education without taking account of the distinctive expertise involved in teaching as 'zero level mentoring' (McIntyre and Hagger, 1993). What is certain is the need to explore, as the Leicester team have done, the similarities and differences in what 'mentoring' means, and what it most helpfully could mean, in different contexts.

One basic facet of mentoring apparently recognized as desirable in all contexts is the need for mentors to establish supportive relationships with their protégés. Whether one looks to the wider literature or to studies of mentoring of teachers in various institutional contexts and at different stages of their careers, good personal relationships are needed in order that mentors can provide the encouragement, support and nurturing which, it seems to be agreed, is at least one of the functions which they should fulfil. The precise terms in which these supportive relationships are seen appears to vary with the context. The Leicester study reports that headteachers saw mentoring predominantly as 'peer support'. Middle managers and NQTs also thought it important that their relationships with their mentors should be non-hierarchical, but they nonetheless stressed the importance of their mentors having greater experience, expertise and knowledge than themselves. In the ITE context, Elliott and Calderhead (1993) are among these who have found mentors frequently using analogies of 'mother–daughter' and 'sisters' to describe these centrally important personal relationships.

Among the conditions seen as necessary for such supportive relationships are the interpersonal skills in dealing with adults emphasized by Campbell and Kane's primary school mentors in Chapter 2, an appropriate 'match' between mentor and protégé, (emphasized, for example, by the headteachers in the Leicester study) and, universally, time for the mentor to be available and therefore to be genuinely supportive.

There also seems to be widespread, although perhaps not universal, agreement that in educational contexts mentoring means both providing constructive and critical advice and challenging practices and preconceptions. In the Leicester study, there appears to have been a generally felt need for this among NQTs and middle managers – although the need was not always met – but not such a wide readiness to accept it as a necessary element of mentoring for headteachers. It is, however, an essential component of the classical image of mentoring, based on Homer's Mentor, with the wise experienced teacher sharing his personal vision and understanding with his protégé through the informal teaching and guidance possible in the context of a personal though far from equal relationship (Smith and Alred, 1993). Bush and his colleagues discuss the possible tension between this aspect of the role and that of providing support, and it certainly seems that this more assertive element of mentoring is more generally found in prescriptions for mentoring than it is in descriptions of mentoring in practice.

These two broad aspects of mentoring, those of 'support' and 'challenge', are what the Leicester team suggest are necessary 'if the mentoring process is to promote professional development'; and, in relation to the inservice contexts which they studied, their analysis is persuasive. On their own, however, these two aspects do not seem adequate to encompass the task of mentoring as it has developed in preservice teacher education. The contrast is strikingly apparent in the Oxford study which explored teachers' conceptions of appropriate provision for student teachers and for NQTs in a school with well-developed provision for both. NQTs were seen *as teachers*, whose learning was incidental to their work, with the appropriate support for their learning being seen as correspondingly marginal and informal. Student teachers on the other hand, even as interns in the school for most of a year, were seen primarily *as learners*, for whose learning extensive, multi-faceted and planned provision should be made.

If the people primarily responsible for making such provision for student teachers in schools are 'mentors', then the concept of mentoring being used here is very different from that defined by the two aspects already discussed. Mentoring in this sense describes a central role in a planned curriculum. It includes responsibilities for curriculum planning, for management of learning experiences involving other teachers and classes, for relating the planned learning in one's own institution to that in other institutions, for formative and summative assessment, and for a considerable variety of deliberate teaching strategies. This then is something which goes far beyond both 'buddy' notions of mentoring and also the informally shared personal wisdom of Mentor-like figures. If initial teacher education is to be serious and largely school-based, then the key school-based figures, whether or not they are labelled 'mentors', will need to be seen primarily as professional teacher educators.

Such a concept of mentoring is apparent for example in the Manchester Metropolitan and Swansea studies reported in Chapters 2 and 3. The primary school mentors who worked with Anne Campbell and Ian Kane were concerned with how they could plan student teachers' curricula in primary schools so as to make accessible to them a range of expertise and experience, and to provide regular opportunities for them to have the undivided attention of class teachers. They were concerned too about appropriate collaboration in the operation of the curriculum both with class teachers in their own schools and with university staff. They were also concerned with issues of subject expertise, the focus of the Swansea study. As Trisha Maynard reports, the mentors in that study were concerned with complex issues about relationships between different kinds of knowledge and values, and with the need for student teachers to be able to generalize their learning to other content and contexts. They increasingly recognized too the need to plan their teaching of student teachers in focused ways, to consider the student teachers' individual starting points but also to assert their own agendas, and to consider the appropriate ordering of different issues for presentation. They too were concerned with problems of effective collaboration with colleagues and with university staff. Thus in both these studies there was a very clear recognition by the mentors of the complex professional tasks with which they were faced in managing student teachers' learning in school.

It is possible then to conceptualize mentoring in three successively more complex ways. At its most basic, mentoring involves a personal relationship in which a relative novice is supported by a more experienced peer in coming to terms with a new role. At a second level, mentoring also involves active guidance, teaching and challenging of the protégé by the mentor, who accordingly needs to claim some expertise, wisdom and authority; and this may make it more difficult to maintain the necessary supportive personal relationship. At a third level, mentoring additionally involves the management and implementation of a planned curriculum, tailored of course to the needs of the individual, and including collaboration with other contributors in one's own and other institutions.

It is not perhaps surprising that each of these conceptions of mentoring appears currently to have gained wide acceptance for the mentoring of different kinds of protégé, distinguished by their status. Thus the most basic concept of mentoring, that of *peer support*, seems to be widely accepted as appropriate for the mentoring of new headteachers by headteachers from other schools: the mentor is clearly not in a hierarchical relationship with the protégé. Mentoring conceived as *personal support, guidance, teaching and challenge* is widely seen as appropriate for qualified and employed teachers, whether NQTs or middle managers, where an emphasis on personal and non-hierarchical relationships is combined somewhat ambiguously with recognition that mentors need to have greater expertise and authority than their protégés, and with a tendency for mentors normally to also have managerial responsibility for their protégés. The third concept of mentoring seems in practice to be accepted as appropriate for student teachers who are neither qualified nor employed as teachers: as learners, they need not only supportive personal relationships and access to the wisdom of experienced practitioners, but also planned and managed school-based curricula. This suggested correspondence is shown diagrammatically in Figure 8.1. It is not suggested that such a correspondence between concepts of mentoring and the positions people occupy is at all inevitable, only that it describes what seems currently to be widely accepted. In these circumstances, although there are important common elements to the different meanings of 'mentoring', there are also clear dangers of confusion in the use of the same term to describe three such different kinds of roles and relationships.

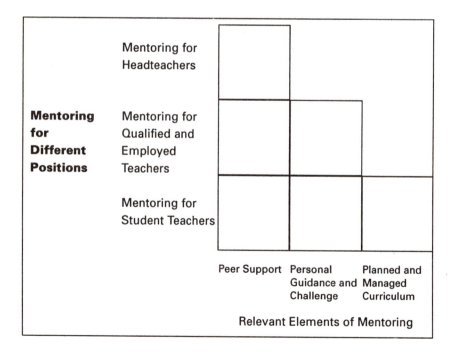

Figure 8.1 Conceptions of mentoring for people in different positions

The mentoring school

The ambitious concept of mentoring outlined above as necessary for school-based ITE suggests that, although responsibility in a school may lie primarily with a co-ordinating professional tutor and specified subject mentors, they are unlikely to be effective unless the school as a whole takes very seriously the implications of its engagement in ITE. It seems clear that effective teacher education will depend on the schools as a whole having thought through and adopted an appropriate policy for ITE, and on many different members of the school staff making informed and mutually complementary contributions to student teachers' learning experiences.

This general claim is supported in relation to secondary schools by the evidence presented in Chapter 5 by Derek Glover and George Mardle. Perhaps the most striking feature of their evidence is the enormous variation which they report among schools – even within the same partnerships – in the use made of resources for ITE, in the degree of integration of planning for ITE with the other work of the school, and in the provision made to support the work of individual mentors. On the basis of their case studies of these widely varying schools, they concluded that the quality of student teachers' learning experiences depended primarily on three main factors:

- the attitude of individual mentors, which in turn depended heavily on their recruitment, training and role satisfaction
- the attitude of the subject department
- the atmosphere for training engendered by the school as a community

Their commentary on the third of these factors is worth repeating.

> Where students are seen as a necessary evil, managed, but not developed, by a professional mentor who is a member of a hard-pressed senior team without either time or recognition for the liaison work necessary, the attitude of the school staff as a whole tends to see the activity as an additional burden often with limited empathy or support for the training process. Where the students are accepted as part of a whole-school policy, and where this work is integrated with the general professional development of staff, our evidence is of positive and productive relationships. In three of the twenty schools studied the 'bolt-on' nature of teacher training was detrimental to the experience of students.

More generally they conclude

> The most successful training environment appears to be that where the senior staff of the school has developed a policy for student training as part of a total staff development policy, negotiated the payment of time and money as part of a total package for involvement, and where the concept of the training school has become part of the culture.

The Oxford study of the relation of ITE to provision for NQTs gives further support to the Keele conclusion that ITE is likely to be most effective where it is an integral part of whole school policy for professional development. Both studies emphasise also the advantages of active professional development leadership, of this whole-school role *not* being the responsibility of a deputy head with many other responsibilities, and of close liaison with heads of subject departments over such professional development work.

This kind of integrated professional development work has to be recognised as increasingly important for schools engaged in ITE, especially if account is also taken of schools' recently increased responsibilities for the induction of NQTs and for the inservice professional education of all staff. It is indeed not too fanciful to see professional development work, led by a core team of a professional tutor and subject mentors, as an emerging third major strand of the work of schools, just as pastoral work emerged as a second clear strand a quarter of a century ago.

The second of the three suggested major influences on the effectiveness of school-based ITE was the attitude of the subject department. The Sussex study reported in Chapter 4 elucidated one element of this influence, the compatibility of the student teacher's view of the subject with the subject ideology dominant in the department. Another important element is the quality of the mentor's liaison with other members of the department in the management of the student teacher's learning experiences. One of the Oxford studies explored the difficulties in such liaison and found them to be substantial and complex. What emerged most clearly from this study is that the individual mentor cannot reasonably be expected to undertake alone the task of mobilising a whole department for ITE work: the head of department, the headteacher and the partner university all also have important responsibilities.

As Glover and Mardle make clear, effective leadership and co-ordination of ITE at a whole school level, and effective leadership and management of student teachers' learning within subject departments, are two different and important factors contributing to the success of ITE in secondary schools. In primary schools these two factors collapse into one: the headteacher's leadership and the mentor's co-ordination and management generally correspond to what is provided at both whole-school and departmental levels in secondary schools. It is not surprising therefore that Campbell and Kane treat 'the mentoring school' as of critical importance at the primary stage.

That structural difference between primary and secondary schools is important. So too is the cross-curricular responsibility and the associated child-centred culture of primary school teachers. In other respects, however, we are not fully convinced that the culture of the mentoring primary school is as different from that of secondary schools as Campbell and Kane suggest. We are more struck indeed by the resonance between their account of mentoring primary schools and the realities, needs and tensions of secondary schools and departments engaged in ITE. Important problems to which they allude which are common in the management of ITE in both primary and secondary schools include the need to maintain the following kinds of balance:

- *between* the need for a climate of explicitness and openness about classroom practice and thinking *and* acceptance of the reality that classrooms remain largely private places with the teaching that goes on in them largely taken for granted and often idiosyncratic;
- *between* the need for mentors' systematic diagnosis of student teachers' needs and management of their learning experiences in relation to an overall planned curriculum *and* recognition of class teachers' conventional right to considerable autonomy in relation to what happens in their classrooms;
- *between* the need for the mentor's position to be one carrying considerable authority *and* the need for the mentor not to have a multiplicity of other responsibilities;
- *between* the need for a substantial proportion of the staff to be actively and seriously engaged in the work of ITE *and* recognition that ITE cannot be more than a very minor aspect of the school's work;
- *between* the need for substantial numbers of staff to be actively and seriously engaged in ITE work *and* recognition that, especially in small schools or departments, not many staff may be well equipped to be so involved;
- *between* the need to stimulate critical reflection in student teachers *and* the need to socialise them into the culture of a school in which working conditions and external demands are not at all conducive to reflection.

So long as these balances need to be delicately maintained it will be difficult – and therefore probably rare – for schools and departments to be effectively mobilised for ITE. Really effective school-based ITE will depend upon altering the realities underlying these problems; and although it is difficult to envisage such fundamental changes being motivated by the needs of ITE alone, there are other factors which may well contribute to change. The possibility of whole-school professional development work becoming increasingly integrated and important is one major possibility which has already been discussed. The corporate planning and evaluation of successive National Curriculum schemes may have contributed in a more than temporary way to changing practices in both primary and secondary schools. Those responsible for ITE should not, however, simply wait for conditions to improve; and it may be that the other members of ITE partnerships have some responsibility in this respect.

Partnership

All the schools involved in the ITE-related studies reported in this book were working in partnership with higher education institutions. In view of this, there is remarkably little mention in the various reports of these partnerships or of the HEIs. It is true that in relation to subject knowledge and beliefs, the issue highlighted in the Swansea and Sussex reports and to be discussed in the next section of this chapter, the part that should be played by the universities is always close to the surface, although even there it is largely implicit. On other issues the silence is almost total, even with regard to the roles of HEI staff in schools. The significance of this large scale silence about HEIs may be indicated by thinking about how unlikely, and how absurd, a similar silence about the schools would be in reports of HEIs initial teacher education scheme. One of the main things that needs to be considered here, therefore, is what this silence means.

The Keele report, however, does explicitly consider views about the three partnerships from which its twenty case study schools were chosen. Among its most interesting findings are those related to schools' involvement in the planning of the partnership schemes. First there is the contrast between Glover and Mardle's own categorisation of fourteen schools as having played a part in this planning and six which for one reason or another did not and, on the other hand, their report that

> staff in thirteen schools appear to think that the framework for operation has been determined by the HEI, four feel that there is a joint planning relationship, and the remaining three feel that the HEI has limited influence because the department or the individual operate in their own way.

Thus the awareness of working in partnership seems very much stronger in the HEIs than in the schools. Also interesting is Glover and Mardle's report that the fourteen schools that had in their view been involved in the planning were very much happier with their relationships with the respective HEIs than were the other six, for which there had been

> a long period of adjustment with difficulties arising from the student profile assessment system, a fundamental misunderstanding by schools of the contractual input of subject tutors, and a misunderstanding of pedagogical requirements.

The Keele report also mentions 'certain barriers to the successful evolution of a partnership', which included schools' perceptions that they were not treated as equals, that they were not adequately funded, and that they were neglected by the HEI especially in coping with marginal students. Schools wanted both to be consulted and to have freedom for 'College guidelines ... to be interpreted in the light of school needs'. Finally, 'there is a general view that the support given by the HEI is appropriate given the contractual arrangements'.

All the above findings – if, as we suspect, they are broadly generalisable – together with the wider silence about HEIs and partnerships, suggest that the arrangements between HEIs and schools are very unequal partnerships, if they can legitimately be called partnerships at all. As seen from the schools, what seems generally to be happening is that the HEIs, preferably taking account of the views of schools, specify requirements and provide some financial resources and whatever limited support they feel they can promise. The schools get on as best they can with the more or less clearly specified task of teacher training. If the HEIs are themselves participating in the work of teacher training, then it is in a largely invisible, or at least a taken-for-granted, way. There is no evidence that mentors and their school-based colleagues feel any need to take account in their own work with student teachers of anything done by the HEIs; nor is there any indication of follow-up by the HEIs of anything done by school staff. From this perspective, then, the partnership looks basically to be one of the universities paying schools to train teachers.

That is certainly not a satisfactory picture: without a substantial, clearly identified and effectively integrated contribution from the universities, school-based ITE is likely to be much weaker than it should be, both in the knowledge made available to student teachers and in the thinking in which they are helped to engage. On the other hand, we should not be too surprised by some of the features of this kind of partnership. Alexander (1990:61) is one of those who have argued convincingly that partnerships for initial teacher education are bound to be unequal in certain respects for the simple reason that, while the training of teachers is a major part of the work of university departments of education, the primary task in which schools are engaged is that of educating children. As he notes, 'there's also something here to be exploited, if you happen to believe that differences in perspective are actually productive.'

In addition, as argued by Crozier *et. al.* (1990), the nature of partnerships could not but be influenced by the political climate within which they were introduced, with an official emphasis on a need for greater practicality being accompanied by widespread attacks on university contributions to ITE. The majority of student teachers, of course, have always 'known' that the important part of their learning happens when they are *doing* teaching in schools. These circumstances make it unsurprising that the planning of teacher education programmes is seen largely as a university responsibility, while schools generally take it for granted that their contributions, embedded in their ongoing busy teaching work, will be viewed as the really important parts of these programmes. Therefore, inadequate as existing partnerships are, we should view them as the predictable starting points from which we have to develop. The possibilities for such development are apparent, for example, from the thoughtful and enthusiastic way in which many mentors collaborated in the work reported in this book.

The nature of the developments in partnership that may be desirable can perhaps be indicated in broad outline through reference to the questions which we raised in the introductory chapter.

How clear are the conditions of the partnership: what is expected of the different partners in terms of what will be done when, and how, and in relation to what criteria of quality?

Given that it is universities who are expected to specify what is required, after appropriate consultation with schools, it is they who have the responsibility for ensuring clarity. Of course flexibility is necessary to take account of the distinctive needs of individual student teachers and the distinctive circumstances of individual schools; but schools greatly welcome clarity and consistency in partnership arrangements. Most of the problems which surface in partnerships, as reflected in the Keele evidence, stem from either lack of consultation or lack of clarity. Furthermore, problems in schools' internal arrangements for ITE can arise from lack of clarity about role expectations, as was the case with regard to the role of subject teachers other than mentors investigated in one of the Oxford studies. As in that case, clear and authoritative guidance from universities will often be seen as important for solving the problems. One of the main ways in which partnerships, and ITE provision more generally, can be improved is through clearer thinking and communication by university departments of education about what they expect to be happening in schools.

What division of labour is seen as being appropriate between universities and schools? And to what extent, and in what ways, is student teachers' work in the two contexts *integrated*?

The important question about division of labour is not 'What elements of the work traditionally done by HEIs should be handed over to schools?', but 'What elements of the expertise that student teachers need as teachers can they develop at least equally well in universities?' Most student teachers will quite rightly judge the usefulness of what they learn in terms of its value for their practice in schools, and it is they who will need to integrate the different things which they learn into their practice in schools. School-based teacher educators are likely to recognise increasingly that they need all their available time to facilitate the learning by student teachers that can only occur in schools. They may also recognise both the value for student teachers' developing practice of ideas from elsewhere – from research, from differing practices, from the student teachers' own reading and writing – and their own need to depend on student teachers gaining access to such ideas through working with university-based teacher educators. However, this is likely only if the university-based teacher educators have clear, consistent and convincing ideas about the division and integration of their respective contributions to the student teachers' learning.

What kinds of *constraints* limit the realisation in practice of theoretical conceptions of the kinds of partnership which should be operating between schools and universities?

Glover and Mardle offer several important answers to this question: the realization of effective partnership is constrained by the failure of universities to treat schools as equal partners, to consult seriously, to provide what is seen as adequate financial resources, and to be available to help in difficult circumstances. It is also constrained by the wide variation in seriousness with which school senior managements treat ITE and by the corresponding variation in mentors' conceptions of their responsibilities. Probably more fundamental, however, is the constraint which results from the widespread failure of universities to commit themselves enthusiastically and intelligently to realizing the major potential for improvement in ITE which partnership with schools could bring. The most damaging constraint of all, of course, is the contamination of the idea of partnership by the widespread perception of it as an irresponsible ideological initiative by the national government. Hope for the future must depend upon establishing the idea of partnership in ITE as a valuable idea for the professional development of teaching, an idea which was however exploited by politicians for their own ideological ends.

Subject knowledge and beliefs

Both the Swansea study reported in Chapter 3 and the Sussex study reported in Chapter 4 are concerned with the ways in which mentors deal with subject-related issues. That apart, their starting points were very different: Trisha Maynard was exploring with subject mentors in primary schools the possibilities and problems of their accepting major responsibilities for student teachers' subject knowledge, while Lisa Dart and Pat Drake were examining the implications of the varying beliefs about their subjects held by secondary school student teachers and their mentors. We would argue that nonetheless many of the issues into which the two studies were led can usefully be seen as related.

Gaps in subject knowledge

In both primary and secondary schools, mentors – especially after some experience and reflection – recognise the considerable importance of gaps in student teachers' prior subject knowledge. Such gaps have been highlighted by the introduction of the National Curriculum. The scale of the problem is indeed such that it is difficult to see how it can effectively be handled: Dart and Drake, dealing with English and mathematics, quote with approval the judgment by Booth *et. al.* (1990) in relation to history that the task is not possible within a one-year PGCE programme. The suggestion that the problem might be dealt with in a school context seemed neither cost-effective in the judgment of the primary mentors nor to be making the best use of their expertise. More fundamentally, such a school-based enterprise, at either primary or secondary level, would it seems inevitably involve a much wider range of subject-related issues such as the uses to be made of subject knowledge, the teaching methods to be adopted, and the philosophies underlying the subject teaching. If gaps in subject knowledge are to be understood and dealt with in a straightforward and simple way, the arguments for dealing with these gaps in the HEI context seem very strong. Experience in schools may however be very important in making student teachers aware of the gaps in their subject knowledge and in motivating them to develop the understandings that they lack.

Kinds of knowledge required for teaching

The primary and secondary studies make it clear that student teachers need to develop many different kinds of subject-related knowledge in order to become effective teachers. Among ways of construing these different kinds of knowledge are the DfE's distinction between subject knowledge and subject application (DfE, 1992, 1993) and Shulman's (1986) distinctions between 'content knowledge', 'pedagogical content knowledge' and 'curriculum knowledge', with subject-related kinds of knowledge being further distinguished in both cases from more general kinds such as 'general pedagogical knowledge'. Both the studies reported in this book also emphasise understanding of the nature of each subject.

It is clear from both studies, however, that mentors find it very difficult in practice to talk about their own knowledge, or about the knowledge needed by student teachers, in ways which differentiate between such various kinds of knowledge and disentangle one kind from another. There seem to be two basic problems with such distinctions. One is that experienced teachers do not in practice find them relevant to their work. The other is that they are based on important assumptions about subjects and about the teaching of subjects with which many teachers would not agree. The categories of knowledge used by the DfE, and those suggested by Shulman, are not based on studies of the nature of teachers' knowledge or of the kinds of thinking that will make teaching most effective. They are based instead on a prescriptive common sense about what teachers 'obviously' ought to do. As such, they are probably quite helpful in reminding all those engaged in teacher education about aspects of student teachers' knowledge which should not be neglected. On the other hand, as a basis for the planning of teacher education curricula or perhaps organising the division of labour between schools and universities, they are likely to be misleading and a source of confusion. Maynard's 'subject mentors' exemplify this point very well: as a result of focusing on subject-related issues, they gained useful understandings about the importance of student teachers' subject knowledge; but in the way they went about this teacher education work, they sensibly rejected the arbitrary imposition of categories which did not reflect the way they approached their own teaching.

Philosophies underlying subject teaching

It is probably in this respect that the biggest difference is apparent between primary and secondary school teachers. For the primary mentors in the Swansea study, subjects had to take second place to their child-centred concerns. For the secondary mentors, on the other hand, it was the philosophy underlying their view of the subject itself that tended to be important. Yet although the specific nature of these underlying philosophies differed between primary and secondary teachers, what is clearly common to the two is that practical approaches to teaching are heavily dependent on such philosophical understandings of the nature of the specific subject knowledge. In the context of initial teacher education, therefore, these underlying philosophies and their implications need to be understood by student teachers; this need is most obvious and most urgent where conflicting philosophies and correspondingly different practices are in evidence.

The need for such examination of underlying subject philosophies is that much the greater in secondary schools because student teachers themselves have their preconceived subject philosophies, usually taken for granted and not at all explicit; these may well be in conflict with the subject philosophies dominant in their host school departments. Dark and Drake also demonstrate, however, that mentors seem to have considerable difficulty in, or perhaps lack of inclination for, discussing subject philosophies with their student teachers. They have relatively little difficulty in discussing the practices of teaching which manifestly embody such philosophies; but they tend to be reluctant or unable to examine the philosophies themselves, abstracted from the processes of teaching. As Dart and Drake comment,

> What is surprising is that through lack of time, or uncertainty about the division of labour between the HEI and schools and the changing role of the mentor, discussion with the trainees about these beliefs seem at best minimal and at worst non-existent.

Why should this be? The suggestions of lack of time and uncertainty about the division of labour with the HEI are both plausible. So too is Dart and Drake's further suggestion that the nature of the power relationship between mentor and trainees is likely to inhibit any attempts by trainees to initiate such discussion. However, evidence from a study by Davies (1993) strongly suggests that the problem is more fundamental. He negotiated with English mentors in the Oxford scheme for such discussions of subject philosophy to be an important part of their school-based role, successfully led the student teachers to engage in enthusiastic debate in the university context about philosophies of English, but nonetheless found that mentors did not themselves initiate, and did not respond to student teachers' efforts to initiate, discussions about different subject philosophies and their implications for practice.

It seems likely that one important factor is the already discussed difficulty for experienced practitioners to disentangle one aspect of their practical knowledge from others: the subject beliefs that inform their practice have become tightly integrated with other elements of their practical expertise, so tightly integrated, perhaps, that they would need to be highly motivated to disentangle it. Also very important, then, are the reasons why mentors may not be so motivated. Among such reasons may be, first, that it is practice itself which seems important to mentors, not intellectual debates about different theoretical ideas for practice and the part of subject philosophies in justifying such theoretical ideas. Second, and closely related, it may be that because experienced teachers' actual processes, and the values and assumptions which underlie them, are defining features of their professional selves, they are likely to feel personally threatened by serious questioning of these practices, values and assumptions. They may understandably feel that it is unacceptable for novices – or university non-practitioners – to threaten them in such a way.

The role of the university

The authors of both the chapters concerned with subject-related issues end by raising important questions about roles within school–university partnerships. Maynard emphasises the importance of such roles being negotiated, the likely connection between universities' increasing concentration on 'practical' issues and the tentative hold student teachers are seen to have on subject principles, and the possible need for HEI tutors' continued involvement in school-based work in order to focus selectively on subject-related knowledge. Dart and Drake ask

> Are there ways that the university can, in conjunction with schools, prepare trainees to think about the underlying beliefs of their subject and enable them to see their influence in the teaching of it?

This focus on the university contribution to the partnership, and those specific points, seem to us entirely right. There are no benefits from partnership if university staff try to pretend that they are 'practical' teachers while at the same time asking real teachers to behave like university academics.

To ask experienced teachers to reveal and explain their own existing practice to student teachers as they themselves think about it, as well as helping the student teachers to develop their practical expertise, is asking a great deal. It is university staff who ought to have the informed expertise necessary for engaging abstractly and analytically with decontextualised thinking and debate about teaching, just as it is necessary to rely upon the expertise of school staff for engaging in and supporting the contextualised practice of teaching. Both kinds of expertise are necessary; but while many *individuals* hold both kinds of expertise, their working conditions in one type of institution or the other makes it unrealistic to expect school mentors or university tutors in general to offer the others' expertise. What precisely that general principle should mean in practice must depend upon serious and open negotiation. But it is surely part of the responsibility of university tutors, as relatively full-time teacher educators, to develop theoretical understandings of what would be realistic and productive roles for mentors and tutors, and thus to offer useful starting points for negotiation.

Resourcing, quality control and benefits for the school

The great advantage of school-based teacher education is that the learning of individual student teachers in real classroom situations can be guided in ways that take account of their individual needs. There is no advantage in placing student teachers in schools or classrooms without any professional educators to take responsibility for them: at best they learn how to survive, meeting their own immediate felt needs but not usually learning how to facilitate pupils' learning. Placed in schools with mentors as their individual professional educators, student teachers can be helped gradually to learn in realistic ways and also in ways which are always directed towards them becoming effective teachers. Mentors can show them, and explain to them, appropriate models to be understood and perhaps emulated; mentors can create the conditions in which they can practise skills and strategies appropriately; mentors can plan and teach alongside them and give them informed feedback (McIntyre 1994). Carefully planned partnerships in which student teachers spend most of their time under the guidance of their mentors in schools could potentially represent a considerable advance in the quality of initial teacher education.

All this depends however on mentors having time to diagnose student teachers' needs, to plan and to negotiate appropriate experiences for them, to observe them, and to work and talk with them. As a system, such *individualised* attention for student teachers is potentially superior to what preceded it, but it is also inherently more expensive. The government have imposed the system, but they have not provided the extra money. It is not surprising therefore that the repeated refrain of almost all investigations of school-based teacher education is that mentors need more time, and more high-quality time, in order to fulfil their role adequately. In addition, there is an increasingly clear need, as reflected in several studies reported here, for other teachers to have time to contribute to the student teachers' learning.

It does not require complicated calculations to demonstrate why there is a problem. The currently accepted rate at the time of writing is for HEIs to pass on to secondary schools £1,000 for hosting a student teacher for two-thirds of an academic year. Ignoring other costs for the school, this represents approximately one twenty-fifth of the average cost of employing a teacher, and so the cost of some fifty hours of a teacher's directed time in a year. Since the co-ordinating professional tutor needs a good deal of time, and since high quality time means regularly timetabled time, a reasonable allowance for a mentor from a financial perspective is one timetabled hour per student throughout the year. That is quite inadequate to allow a mentor to provide the kinds of support and teaching which most student teachers need.

At the same time, mentors and student teachers are generally receiving, as a result of the new financial arrangements, much less support from universities than was previously normal. Universities vary in their financial circumstances and in their attitudes, and they have varied in their support for teacher education partnerships with schools. The possibilities for variation are dramatic. Wiliam (1994), for example, has shown that the money available for the university staffing of a PGCE course, after the payment of £1,000 per student to schools has been made, could be so small as to make the course obviously non-viable or, at the opposite extreme, could involve only about a twenty per cent reduction on previous staffing for the course, depending on how the university chooses to make the calculations. Since the students do, under the new arrangements, spend most of their time in schools, and therefore make limited use of university accommodation, libraries, computers and other services, universities should reasonably be expected to tend towards the latter of these options.

University departments of education themselves, however, have choices to make. The extent to which departmental incomes can depend on their research ratings makes it very attractive for departments to devote a large proportion of staff time to research and much less to initial teacher education work than previously. The aspect of ITE that is most time-consuming, and therefore the biggest potential source of time-saving, is tutors' time spent with mentors and with student teachers in schools. Some university departments of education are saving a great deal of time in that area. This, in addition to the shortage of time, is likely to undermine the quality of mentors' work and of student teachers' school-based learning. As noted in the Keele study, the most stressful, time-consuming and professionally demanding aspect of a mentor's work can often be the task of providing support for weak student teachers (and also perhaps ultimately failing them). It is with such work that mentors often most want and need the help of university tutors. Secondly, all schools and mentors have a great deal still to learn about school-based initial teacher education and they deserve the support of their university partners in such learning. In addition, if a student teacher is not getting adequate support from his or her mentor, the university tutor needs to compensate for this to some degree through regular visits.

There are, then, serious questions to be asked about the quality of some university contributions to ITE partnerships. There are also, as documented by Glover and Mardle in Chapter 5, wide variations in the quality of schools' contributions, so wide indeed that they concluded that the professional education being provided by some of their case study schools was unsatisfactory. Issues of quality control are important on both sides of the partnerships. Such issues would be delicate in any case between partners more accustomed to working in a spirit of voluntary professionalism, with tactful withdrawal from working together as an adequate sanction. They are however extremely difficult in circumstances where doing what the available money pays for is professionally not good enough. There would be no problem in articulating the performance indicators for assessing minimally satisfactory contributions; but implementing a system for the use of such performance indicators might not be acceptable in the present financial circumstances.

In such a situation, most professional institutions which combine seriousness about ITE with good reputations are still able to withdraw from particular unsatisfactory partnerships when necessary, and ultimately to withdraw from ITE itself without significant financial loss. It is however the national government which must accept general responsibility, and the way forward for any government which cares about the quality of school teaching is clear: the provision of adequate increased funding for ITE would allow it to demand quality assurance and control mechanisms to ensure consistently high standards.

While the present unsatisfactory financial situation lasts, it is likely that schools will continue to participate in ITE, and to take it seriously, only if there are benefits in it for them other than the financial. It is reassuring therefore that several of the studies reported here have provided evidence of such benefits.

For schools, the primary concern will generally be with whether pupils benefit or lose from the school's commitment to ITE. This is not an easy question to investigate and there has been correspondingly little systematic study of it. The small-scale Oxford study reported in Chapter 6 does however support more informal impressions that pupils get more adult help, more variety in their lessons, and more carefully prepared lessons as a result of competent school-based ITE. The pupils themselves were in no doubt that they benefited considerably. The difference between the two departments studied is also worthy of note: the department in which there was integrated planning for ITE, with the involvement of all teachers, was the one in which pupils' perception of benefit was most absolute. In the department where student teachers 'just got on with it' with the classes of teachers other than their mentor, the pupils' enthusiasm was more qualified. Glover and Mardle noted similar differences among schools: those whose ITE efforts were 'co-ordinated' reported that the 'additional staff in the classroom...increases pupil support' and 'the possibility of additional input for assessment, team teaching, project and individual work' were among the benefits they gained. It surely ought to be the case that where student teachers are being given the kinds of task and the degrees of autonomy most suitable for their own learning, pupils will generally benefit too.

Benefits for teachers, more varied and more widely documented elsewhere, are commented on in most of the chapters of this book, as well as in the Oxford study that focused on such benefits. The additional help of student teachers can make space, and the new ideas they bring with them can provide stimulus, for individual or corporate development. Primary and secondary schools seemed to welcome the links with HEIs, and the educational opportunities as well as the opportunities for accreditation of training that these provided. The mentors participating in the Oxford study emphasised especially intrinsic benefits from mentoring – the management skills developed, the opportunity for a new dimension to one's professional life, and especially the stimulus to reflect on one's own practices and expertise. Such professional development benefits tend to depend, as Maynard also notes, on the attributes of mentors themselves and also on the support of headteachers.

It seems clear that if such various kinds of benefits were consistently realized within a school, then the advantages of engagement in ITE would be likely to outweigh the inadequacy of the financial resources provided. And it seems clear too that the schools which invest their own energies into ITE most fully, and plan for it most professionally, tend to be those which derive the greatest benefit. However, neither university departments of education nor the government should be reassured by the knowledge of such possible benefits for schools: without high quality schemes led by university departments, and without adequate resourcing from the government, the quality of initial teacher education will continue to be highly variable.

Developing mentoring

What conditions and support are necessary to enable mentors to develop the confidence and the expertise to shape and develop their own roles? That, we suggested in our introduction, is perhaps the most fundamental question. It is so because mentoring, like teaching, can only be a successful activity if those who are engaged in it are deeply committed to it and confident in its value and feasibility.

We suggest below six conditions for such shaping by mentors of their own roles. The importance of these conditions has been indicated by the evidence and arguments of this book, and also by wider experience.

1. *Mentors need to be working in partnership with university staff who*
are enthusiastic about the move towards school-based teacher education and see that move as a way of solving endemic problems in ITE. This implies that university-based teacher educators should have developed a good theoretical understanding of these problems. It is necessary because these other teacher educators, with well established university bases, are mentors' natural allies, needed to assert the importance of mentors' demanding work.

recognize mentors as equal partners in ITE on the basis of their expertise as practising teachers and of their ongoing work in particular school settings. Mentors' confidence in their own capacity to shape their role appropriately must depend on their confident belief that their expertise and work as practising teachers is recognized as the crucial basis for their role, and as equally important for initial teacher education as academically based knowledge.

offer tentative negotiable plans for teacher education curricula which are soundly based on well theorised understandings of beginning teachers' learning and of mentors' situations and expertise. These curriculum plans should emphasise practical ideas for the division of labour between, and the integration of, university and school contributions. There is still a great need for coherently theorised curricula within which mentors can work. Mentors' capacities to shape their own roles will be much greater if they can start from curricular (as opposed to merely administrative) plans which are intelligently based on clear and contestable understandings.

2. *Mentors need more time* than most of them currently have, in order that they can undertake their role in a thoughtful, professional and developmental way. For example, three or four hours per week of regularly timetabled time, for a mentor with two student teachers (some of which could sometimes be offered to colleagues working with the student teachers) would be an efficient way of using a modest increase to current resourcing. To some extent this depends on effective partnership

and school planning, but primarily it must depend on increased government expenditure on ITE, and on responsible government (or TTA) planning for the use of these resources.

3. ***Mentors need established positions within well-structured and clearly recognized whole-school frameworks.*** With current arrangements, there is frequently too much ambiguity about the status of mentors, and mentors too often have to work in isolation. Headteachers generally need to give much fuller consideration to the way in which professional development responsibilities are structured – across stages in teachers' careers and across departments – with strong whole-school leadership, but taking account of the key roles of heads of department. The development of school pastoral teams might, at its best, provide a helpful model for the development of school professional development teams, within which mentors would be key people.

4. ***Mentors need support to explore different aspects of their roles.*** This book has offered examples of mentors identifying questions that needed investigation, and of mentors having the time and opportunity to explore new possibilities, and of mentors collaborating in the investigation of problems they faced and of possible solutions to these problems. All aspects of mentoring need to be questioned and explored by mentors in such ways. There is a need for widespread and sustained support, in terms of both time and structured opportunities for teamwork and consultation. The government need to follow the lead given by the Esmée Fairbairn Charitable Trust, and make resources available so that mentors can take further steps towards their informed ownership of their own school-based teacher education work.

References

Alexander, R. (1984) *Primary Teaching*, Eastbourne: Holt, Rinehart and Winston.

Alexander, R. (1990) Partnership in initial teacher education: confronting the issues, in M. Booth, J. Furlong and M.Wilkin (eds), *Partnership in Initial Teacher Training*, London: Cassell, pp. 59–73.

Alexander, R., Rose, J. and Woodhead, C. (1992) *Curriculum Organisation and Classroom Practice in Primary Schools*, London: HMSO.

Archer, M.F.W. and Hogbin, J. (1990) The new teacher in school. Interim Report 1989/1990, Didsbury School of Education, Manchester Polytechnic.

Argyris, C. and Schön, D. (1974) *Theory in Practice: Increasing Professional Effectiveness*, San Francisco: Jossey-Bass.

Bark, A. (1994), Newly qualified teachers: their induction and professional development. Unpublished MA dissertation, University of Leicester.

Becher, T. (1989) *Academic Tribes and Territories*, Milton Keynes: Open University Press.

Berrill, M. (1992), Structured mentoring and the development of teaching skill, in M. Wilkin (ed.), *Mentoring in Schools*, London: Kogan Page.

Bolam, R., McMahon A., Pocklington, K. and Weindling D., (1994) Headteacher mentoring: a route to effective school management. Paper presented at the annual meeting of the American Educational Research Association, 4–8 April, New Orleans.

Booth, M., Shawyer, G. and Brown, R. (1990) Partnership and the training of student history teachers, in M. Booth, J. Furlong and M. Wilkin (eds), *Partnership in Initial Teacher Training*, London: Cassell, pp. 99–109.

Boydell, D. (1994) Developing a collegial approach to teacher education. *Mentoring: Partnership in Teacher Education*, 1(3):312.

Bush, T. (1995) Mentoring for principals: pre-service and in-service models. *Singapore Journal of Education*, 15(1): 1–13.

Calderhead, J. (1988) The development of knowledge structures in learning to teach, in J. Calderhead (ed.) *Teachers' Professional Learning*, Lewes: Falmer, pp. 51–64.

Calderhead, J. and Robson, M. (1991) Images of teaching: student teachers' early conceptions of classroom practice. *Teaching and Teacher Education*, 7(1).

Campbell, A. (1994a) Headteachers talking: primary school headteachers' views on school-based teacher training. *Mentoring in Schools: Interim Research Report no. 5*, Manchester Metropolitan University.

Campbell, A. (1994b) Mentors and mentoring. *Mentoring In Schools Interim Research Report no. 3*, Manchester Metropolitan University.

Campbell, A. and Kane, I.S. (1993) Mentors and mentor training. *Mentoring: Partnership in Teacher Education*, 1(1):16–22.

Carmin, C. (1988) The term mentor: a review of the literature and a pragmatic suggestion. *International Journal of Mentoring*, 2(2): 9–13.

Chong, K.C., Low, G.T. and Walker, A. (1989) *Mentoring: A Singapore Contribution*, Singapore Educational Administration Society.

Clutterbuck, D. (1992) *Mentoring*, Henley: Henley Distance Learning.

Collison, J. (1994) The impact of primary school practices on student experience of mentoring. Paper presented at BERA Conference, September.

Cooper, B. (1990) PGCE students and investigational approaches in secondary maths. *Research Papers in Education*, 5(2):127–151.

Crosson, M. and Shiu, C. (1994) Evaluation and judgement, in B. Jaworski and A. Watson, (eds) *Mentoring in Mathematics Teaching*, Lewes: Falmer Press for the Mathematical Association.

Crozier, G., Menter, I., and Pollard, A. (1990) Changing partnership, in M. Booth, J. Furlong and M. Wilkin (eds), *Partnership in Initial Teacher Training*, London: Cassell, pp. 44–56.

Daresh, J.C. and Playko, M.A. (1992), Mentoring for headteachers: a review of major issues. *School Organisation*, 12(2): 145–152.

Dart, L. and Drake, P. (1993) School-based training: a conservative practice? *Journal of Education for Teaching*, 19(2): 175–189.

Davies, C.W.R. (1993) Ideologies of the subject and the professional training of English teachers. Unpublished PhD thesis, University of Oxford.

DES (1984) *Initial Teacher Training: Approval of Courses*, (Circular 3/84), London: DES.

DES (1989) *Initial Teacher Training: Approval of Courses*, (Circular 24/89), London: DES.

DfE (1992) *Initial Teacher Training of Secondary School Teachers*, Circular 9/92, London: HMSO.

DfE (1993) *Initial Training of Primary School Teachers: New Criteria for Courses*, Circular 14/93, London: HMSO.

Drake, P. and Dart, L. (1994) English, mathematics and mentors, in I. Reid, (ed.). *Teacher Education Reform: Current Research*, London: Paul Chapman.

Dunne, R. and Harvard, G. (1993) A model of teaching and its implications for mentoring, in D. McIntyre, H. Hagger. and M. Wilkin, (eds) (1993) *Mentoring: Perspectives on School-Based Teacher Education*, London: Kogan Page, pp. 117–129.

Eagleton, T. (1983) *Literary Theory: An Introduction*, Oxford: Blackwell.

Earley, P. and Fletcher-Campbell, F. (1989) *The Time to Manage?* Windsor: NFER-Nelson.

Earley, P. and Kinder, K. (1994) *Initiation Rights: Effective Induction Practices for New Teachers*, London: NFER.

Elliott, B. and Calderhead, J. (1993) Mentoring for teacher development: possibilities and caveats, in D. McIntyre, H. Hagger and M. Wilkin (eds), *Mentoring: Perspectives on School-based Teacher Education*, London: Kogan Page, pp. 166–189

Elliott, J. (1991) A model of teacher professionalism and its implications for teacher education. *British Educational Research Journal*, 17(4): 309–318.

Eraut, M. (1994) *Developing Professional Knowledge and Competence*. Lewes: Falmer Press

Evans, C. (1993) *English People*, Milton Keynes: Open University Press.

Featherstone, B. and Smith, S. (1992) Peer support as the basis of good mentoring practice, in M. Wilkin (ed.) *Mentoring in Schools*, London: Kogan Page.

Field, B. (1994) The new role of the teacher–mentor, in B. Field and T. Field (eds), *Teachers as Mentors: A Practical Guide*, London: Falmer Press, pp. 63–77.

Finn, R. (1993) Mentoring: the effective route to school-based development, in H. Green (ed.), *The School Management Handbook*, London: Kogan Page, pp. 151–154.

Fullan, M. (1991) *The New Meaning of Educational Change*, London: Cassell.

Furlong, J. and Maynard, T. (1995) *Mentoring Student Teachers: The Growth of Professional Knowledge*, London: Routledge.

Furlong, J., Whitty, G., Barrett, E., Barton, L. and Miles, S. (1994), Integration and partnership in initial teacher education – dilemmas and possibilities. *Research Papers in Education*, 9(3): 281–309.

Furlong, V.J., Hirst, P.H., Pocklington, K. and Miles, S. (1988) *Initial Teacher Training and the Role of the School*, Milton Keynes: Open University Press.

Gerholm, T. (1985) On tacit knowledge in academia, in L. Gustavson (ed.), *On Communication: No 3*, Linköping: University of Linköping Department of Communication Studies.

Glover, D., Gough, G. and Johnson, M. (1994) Towards a taxonomy of mentoring. *Mentoring and Tutoring*, 2(2): 25–30.

Grubb Institute (1993) *East Midlands Nine Mentors Handbook*, London: Grubb Institute.

Hagger, H., Burn, K. and McIntyre, D. (1993) *The School Mentor Handbook*, London: Kogan Page.

Holly, P. and Southworth, G. (1989) *The Developing School*, London: Falmer Press.

Hustler, D., Peckett, J. and Whiteley, M. (in press) (eds) *Learning Contracts and Initial Teacher Education*, London: David Fulton.

Jacques, K. (1992) Mentoring in initial teacher training. *Cambridge Journal of Education*, 22(3): 337–350.

Jacques, K. (1995) Mentoring in initial teacher education, in T. Kerry, and A. S. Mayes, (eds), *Issues in Mentoring*, London: Routledge, pp. 111–119.

Joyce, B. and Showers, B. (1980), Improving in-service training: the messages of research. *Educational Leadership*, February: 379–385.

Kane, I.S. (1994) Parents and governors: a study by primary school mentors of views on school-based teacher training. *Mentoring in Schools Interim Research Report 4*, Manchester Metropolitan University.

Kelly, M., Beck, A. and Wilkin, M. (1992) Mentoring as staff development activity, in J. apThomas (ed.) *Mentoring in Schools*, London: Kogan Page.

Kelly, M., Beck, T., and apThomas, J. (1992), Mentoring as a staff development activity in M. Wilkin (ed.), *Mentoring in Schools*, London: Kogan Page, pp. 173–180.

Kemmis, S. (1980) The imagination of the case and the invention of the study, in H. Simons (ed.), *Towards A Science of the Singular*, Norwich: University of East Anglia.

Kram, K. (1983) Phases of the mentor relationship. *Academy of Management Journal*, 26: 608–625.

Lawlor, S. (1990) *Teachers Mistaught: Training in Theories or Education in Subjects,* London: Centre for Policy Studies.

Little, J.W. (1990) Teachers as colleagues, in A. Leiberman, (ed.), *Schools as Collaborative Cultures*, London: Falmer Press.

Lortie, D. (1975) *School Teacher: A Sociological Study*, Chicago: University of Chicago Press.

McCulloch, M. and Locke, N.(1994) Mentorship developments in the primary phase of initial teacher education at the University of Reading. *Mentoring: Partnership in Teacher Education*, 1(3): 21–28.

McIntyre, D. (1994) Classrooms as learning environments for beginning teachers, in M. Wilkin and D. Sankey (eds), *Collaboration and Transition in Initial Teacher Training*, London: Kogan Page, pp. 81–93.

McIntyre, D. and Hagger, H. (1993) Teachers' expertise and models of mentoring, in D. McIntyre, H. Hagger and M. Wilkin (eds), *Mentoring: Perspectives on School-based Teacher Education,* London: Kogan Page, pp. 86–115.

McIntyre, D. and Hagger, H. (1994) *Mentoring in Initial Teacher Education: An Overview and Synthesis of Five Research Studies*, London: Paul Hamlyn Foundation.

McIntyre, D., Hagger, H. and Wilkin, M. (eds) (1993) *Mentoring: Perspectives on School-based Teacher Education*, London: Kogan Page.

Maynard, T. (in press) The limits of mentoring: the contribution of the higher education institution tutor to primary student teachers' school-based learning, in J. Furlong and R. Smith (eds), *The Role of Higher Education*, London: Kogan Page.

Maynard, T. and Furlong, J. (1993) Learning to teach and models of mentoring, in D. McIntyre, H.Hagger, and M. Wilkin (eds), *Mentoring: Perspectives on School-Based Teacher Education*, London: Kogan Page, pp. 69–85.

Nias, J. (1989) *Staff Relationships in the Primary School: A Study of Organisational Cultures*, London: Cassell.

O'Hear, A. (1986) *Who Teaches the Teachers?* London: Social Affairs Unit.

O'Neill,J., Middlewood,D. and Glover,D. (1994) *Human Resource Management in Schools and Colleges*, Harlow: Longman.

Pedlar, M., Boydell, T. and Burgoyne, J. (1989) Towards a Learning Company. *Management Education and Development*, 2(1): 1–8.

Rothwell, S., Nardi, E. and McIntyre, D. (1994) The perceived value of the role activities of mentors and curricular, professional and general tutors, in I. Reid, H.Constable, and R.Griffiths (eds), *Teacher Education Reform: Current Research*, London: Paul Chapman, pp. 13–34.

Russell, T. (1988) From pre-service teacher education to first year of teaching: a study of theory and practice, in J. Calderhead (ed.), *Teachers' Professional Learning*, Lewes: Falmer Press, pp. 13–34.

Ruthven, K. (1993) Pedagogical knowledge and the training of mathematics teachers. *Mathematics Review* 3:113–115.

Sanders, S. E. (1994) Mathematics and mentoring, in B. Jaworski, and A. Watson (eds), *Monitoring in Mathematics Teaching*, Lewes: Falmer Press for the Mathematics Association.

School Management Task Force (1990) *Developing School Management: The Way Forward*, London: HMSO.

School Teacher Review Board (1993) *Annual Report*, London: DFE.

Shaw, R. (1992) *Teacher Training in Secondary Schools*, London: Kogan Page.

Showers, B. (1985) Teachers coaching teachers. *Educational Leadership*, 42(7):43–49.

Shulman, L. (1986), Those who understand: knowledge growth in teaching. *Educational Researcher*, 15(2): 4–14.

Smith, R. and Alred, G. (1993) The impersonation of wisdom, in D. McIntyre, H. Hagger and M.Wilkin (eds), *Mentoring: Perspectives on School-based Teacher Education,* London: Kogan Page, pp. 103–116.

Southworth, G. (1994) Mentoring and newly qualified teachers. *Newsletter*, no. 28, Autumn/Winter, University of Cambridge Institute of Education.

Stanulis, R.N. (1994) Fading to a whisper: one mentor's story of sharing her wisdom without telling answers. *Journal of Teacher Education*, 45(1):31–38.

Thomson, R. (1993) *Managing People*, Oxford: Butterworth–Heinemann.

Torrington, D. and Weightman, J. (1989) *The Reality of School Management*, Oxford: Blackwell.

Trethowan, D. (1991) *Managing with Appraisal*, London: Paul Chapman.

UCET (Universities Council for The Education of Teachers) (1994) Circular to HEIs and school partners.

Wall, M. and Smith, P. (1993) Mentoring and newly qualified teachers, in P. Smith and J. West-Burnham (eds), *Mentoring in the Effective School*, Harlow: Longman, pp. 40–65.

Wallace, M. (1991), *School-centred Management Training*, London: Paul Chapman.

West-Burnham, J. (1993) Mentoring and management development, in P. Smith, and J.West-Burnham (eds), *Mentoring in the Effective School*, Harlow: Longman, pp. 124–138.

Wiliam, D. (1994) I'm sorry, but there's not enough money for a third teaching practice visit, in I.Reid, H.Constable and R.Griffiths (eds), *Teacher Education Reform: Current Research,* London: Paul Chapman, pp. 76–86.

Wilkin, M. (ed.) (1992) *Mentoring in Schools*, London: Kogan Page.

Index